SECOND EDITION

Complete Advanced

Workbook **without** answers

Laura Matthews

Barbara Thomas

CAMBRIDGE
UNIVERSITY PRESS

University Printing House, Cambridge CB2 8BS, United Kingdom

One Liberty Plaza, 20th Floor, New York, NY 10006, USA

477 Williamstown Road, Port Melbourne, VIC 3207, Australia

314–321, 3rd Floor, Plot 3, Splendor Forum, Jasola District Centre, New Delhi – 110025, India

103 Penang Road, #05-06/07, Visioncrest Commercial, Singapore 238467

Cambridge University Press is part of the University of Cambridge.

It furthers the University's mission by disseminating knowledge in the pursuit of education, learning and research at the highest international levels of excellence.

www.cambridge.org
Information on this title: www.cambridge.org/9781107631489

© Cambridge University Press 2014

This publication is in copyright. Subject to statutory exception and to the provisions of relevant collective licensing agreements, no reproduction of any part may take place without the written permission of Cambridge University Press.

First published 2009
Second edition 2014

20

Printed in Poland by Opolgraf

A catalogue record for this publication is available from the British Library

ISBN 978-1-107-63106-9 Student's Book without answers with CD-ROM
ISBN 978-1-107-67090-7 Student's Book with answers with CD-ROM
ISBN 978-1-107-69838-3 Teacher's Book with Teacher's Resources CD-ROM
ISBN 978-1-107-63148-9 Workbook without answers with Audio CD
ISBN 978-1-107-67517-9 Workbook with answers with Audio CD
ISBN 978-1-107-64450-2 Class Audio CDs (2)
ISBN 978-1-107-66289-6 Presentation Plus

Cambridge University Press has no responsibility for the persistence or accuracy of URLs for external or third-party internet websites referred to in this publication, and does not guarantee that any content on such websites is, or will remain, accurate or appropriate. Information regarding prices, travel timetables, and other factual information given in this work is correct at the time of first printing but Cambridge University Press does not guarantee the accuracy of such information thereafter.

Contents

1	Our people	4
2	Mastering languages	9
3	All in the mind	14
4	Just the job!	19
5	Dramatic events	24
6	Picture yourself	29
7	Leisure and entertainment	34
8	Media matters	39
9	At top speed	44
10	A lifelong process	49
11	Being somewhere else	54
12	The living world	59
13	Health and lifestyle	64
14	Moving abroad	69
	Acknowledgements	74

1 Our people

Grammar
Verb forms to talk about the past

1 Read part of a story about a woman returning home and then put the verbs in brackets into the correct past tense.

As Anne drove west, she (1) ......felt...... (feel) almost as though she were driving in a dream. But as she (2) .... (get) closer to home, there was an excitement she (3) .... (not experience) for years. She (4) .... (live) abroad for so long that she (5) .... (forget) what it was like to feel that you really belonged somewhere. Her family were there, in her village, and they (6) .... (wait) for her. As she (7) .... (come) over the hill, the view (8) .... (be) the same as it (9) .... (always / be). She noticed a young man who (10) .... (walk) purposefully towards the centre of the village. As the car drew near, he (11) .... (turn) and (12) .... (nod) as people do in this part of the world. She (13) .... (not realise) until then that it was Niall, a boy she (14) .... (babysit) many times when she was a teenager. So not everything (15) .... (stay) the same. Anne herself (16) .... (also / change) of course. The night before, she (17) .... (stay) in a hotel in Dublin and the receptionist (18) .... (ask) her '(19) .... (you / be) to Ireland before?' But what could she expect when her accent (20) .... (almost / disappear)?

2 Read each pair of sentences and then answer the question which follows.

1 A Katrina studied Portuguese when she arrived in Brazil.
   B Katrina has been studying Portuguese since she arrived in Brazil.
   In which sentence is Katrina still in Brazil? ......B......

2 A My brother was always borrowing my things when we were teenagers.
   B My brother always borrowed my things when we were teenagers.
   In which sentence does the speaker seem slightly irritated? ....

3 A Has Richard rung this morning?
   B Did Richard ring this morning?
   In which sentence is it still morning? ....

4 A My school team won the regional championship five times.
   B My school team has won the regional championship five times since 1997.
   In which sentence does the speaker think the team might win the regional championship again? ....

5 A When Giulia got home, her friends made her a meal.
   B When Giulia got home, her friends had made her a meal.
   In which sentence was the meal ready when Giulia arrived? ....

Used to

3 Look at the past tense verbs in these sentences. Rewrite any sentence where the verb can be replaced by *used to*. Write 'No' for any sentence that cannot be changed.

1 ~~Were parents~~ *Did parents use to be* stricter with their children fifty years ago, do you think?
2 After I left school, I went abroad twice to work as an au pair.
3 People wrote letters by hand or on a typewriter until computers became widespread.
4 Is lunch still as important in your country as it was?
5 My father has worked in several different countries so I've been to lots of different schools.
6 I spent last summer helping my grandparents decorate their house.
7 Did you get as stressed at your last job as you do here?
8 I speak Russian quite well as I studied it for four years.
9 Japanese people didn't eat as much chicken in the past as they do now.
10 Wasn't there a factory on this site until a few years ago?

Used to and be/get used to

4 *Used to* and *be/get used to* have different meanings and forms. Look at these sentences written by exam candidates. Find the mistake in each one and then correct it.

1 The children hate walking because they are ~~use~~ *used* to going everywhere by car.
2 Some students are used to eat a snack during classes.
3 Hockey didn't used to be very popular in Spain.
4 Even if you find joining a new school difficult at first, you will soon get used to.
5 Were you used to work under pressure in your old job?
6 If you do not used to walking every day, you will find a trekking holiday very difficult.
7 Have you got used to cook for yourself?
8 José use to be a good swimmer when he was younger.
9 Travel helps you be used to different ways of doing things.
10 Laura was used to have a lot of noise around her because she came from a big family.

Vocabulary
Adjectives describing personality

1 Choose one word from the box to fit in the gap in each sentence. There are two words that don't fit anywhere.

> competent   conscientious   genuine   idealistic
> insensitive   ~~modest~~   outgoing   protective
> self-centred   unconventional

1 You should tell everyone about the prize you won – you're much too ....*modest*......... .
2 Jamie is very .... about making sure he does a job properly and to the best of his ability.
3 My Spanish isn't brilliant but I'm .... enough to write an email or book a hotel.
4 Peter is so .... to those around him that he doesn't even notice when he upsets someone.
5 Many of us are .... when we're young and think we can change the way the world works .
6 My brother is extremely .... and simply loves meeting new people.
7 Anna is a very .... person; you can always trust that she means what she says.
8 Joanna has always been extremely .... of her little brother because he is several years younger than her.

Collocations with *give*, *do* and *make*

2 Look at these sentences written by exam candidates and then choose the correct verb.

1 Our college [gives]/ *makes* us a wide choice of subjects to study.
2 The students were asked to *give / make* their opinions about the new menu in the canteen.
3 We *do / make* a lot of business with American companies.
4 The politician asked the newspaper to *do / make* an apology for the inaccuracies in their report.
5 I have *done / made* hundreds of exercises on grammar and vocabulary this week.
6 We can *give / make* a discount to our regular customers.
7 The strike didn't *do / make* any harm to local businesses.
8 Silva *gave / made* a remark about her sister which I thought was a bit unkind.
9 The college hopes to *do / make* a profit by selling its magazine.
10 The bus company has *done / made* improvements to the services it offers.
11 It is too late to repair some of the damage *done / made* to the environment.
12 It is worth *doing / making* an effort to look back at what you've learnt.
13 Nowadays both men and women *do / make* the housework but it wasn't like that in the past.
14 You will have to *do / make* your own bed every morning while you are living here.
15 The band *gave / made* the best performance of their lives last night.

Reading and Use of English | Part 5

You are going to read an extract from an autobiography. For questions **1–6**, choose the answer (**A**, **B**, **C** or **D**) which you think fits best according to the text.

A visit Home

Amid the swarming, clattering travellers, railway staff and suitcases, I saw the thick, dark eyebrows of my brother Guy lift by approximately one millimetre in greeting as I came down the steps of the footbridge and out into the station forecourt. Guy speaks like most men in the village we come from, i.e. not at all until he has spent five minutes considering whether there are other means of communication he can use instead. His favourites are the eyebrow-raise, the shrug, and the brief tilt of his chin; if he is feeling particularly emotional, he may perform all three together. That morning, as I worked my bags through the other passengers, he kept his eyebrows raised. Standing in his work clothes, he looked rather out of place, resembling a large, solitary rusty nail in the midst of, but apart from, the crowd of people: his steel-capped boots, battered, formless jacket and heavy stubble seemed to be causing many people to give him a wide berth, diverting their path to the exit rather than heading for it directly.

Richard Benson: author of extract 'A visit home'.

'Hello, Guy,' I said.

'Now then,' he replied. 'Give me one of your bags.'

'Thank you,' I said, and passed him a large bag.

'Whatever have you got in here?' he exclaimed.

My brother is appalled by indulgences such as luggage, although his exclamations are less aggressive than resignedly bemused. With Guy, you have to understand that when he asks what on earth you've got in a bag, it is a way of saying, 'Hello, how are you?'

'It'll be the computer that's heavy. And there are some books,' I explained.

'Books,' he said wearily, shaking his head.

'Sorry.'

'Doesn't matter,' he said. 'It's not that heavy.' He yanked the bag up onto his shoulder.

'It's nice to see you, Guy.'

Guy raised his eyebrows and chin five millimetres, and strode off towards the car park.

I felt relieved by his distracted, unemotional expression because it was usual: since he was a small child he had gone through much of life looking as if he was pondering the answer to a complex mathematical problem. But as I caught up with him and looked at him from the side, I noticed dark half-circles below his eyes.

'Are you all right, then?' I said.

He raised his eyebrows again, and blew out through pursed lips. He looked as if he were trying to pop the features off his face. Then he gave me the sort of consolation smile you give people when they've asked a stupid question, batted his lashy black-brown eyes and shrugged.

'You look a bit worn out,' I said.

'I should think I do,' he said. 'I've been doing twelve-hour days on the farm since July. Sling your bags into the back of the van then.'

This was not as straightforward as he made it sound. He used the van as a workshop, storage unit and mobile home, and so as well as the usual driving-dregs of sweet wrappers and plastic bottles, there was farm equipment of an often surprising scale – straw bales, black polythene barrels, bundles of shovels and forks, metal toolboxes which were themselves almost as large as small cars, and other tools which I did not recognise or understand. Intermingled with that were random, inexplicable household articles: sofa cushions, half a dozen plant pots and a roll of carpet.

It takes only twenty minutes to drive through the hills to our village, but that day the journey seemed to take forever. Neither of us could think of anything to say to each other so Guy pretended to concentrate on the speed of his windscreen wipers which were keeping the driving rain off the windscreen so he could see the road ahead. I, on the other hand, leant my forehead against the side window, looking out at the scenery which was so familiar to me but was actually obliterated by the horizontal rain.

1 What aspect of Guy's personality is the writer reinforcing when he says 'if he is feeling particularly emotional, he may perform all three together' (lines 12-13)?
   A His facial expressions are difficult to interpret.
   B His speech is always backed up by non-verbal expressions.
   C He is very controlled when expressing his feelings.
   D He can give out conflicting messages about what he is thinking.

2 What is meant by many people giving Guy 'a wide berth' (line 19)?
   A People were staring at him because of the way he looked.
   B People were getting annoyed with him because he was in their way.
   C People did not understand what he was doing there.
   D People did not feel comfortable getting too close to him.

3 How does the writer feel when Guy complains about his bag?
   A He knows he shouldn't take the complaint seriously.
   B He thinks Guy is making an unnecessary fuss.
   C He wishes Guy had not greeted him with a complaint.
   D He is embarrassed about bringing so much luggage.

4 As they walk towards the car park, the writer realises that
   A he is not being sensitive enough about Guy's situation.
   B there is a change in Guy's normal behaviour.
   C Guy's expression seems more worried than usual.
   D he had more reason to be concerned about Guy than he initially thought.

5 What does the writer exaggerate when he is describing the back of the van?
   A the combination of items
   B the size of some of the contents
   C how old some of the contents were
   D how many items were unnecessary

6 What does the writer say about the journey in the van?
   A He preferred to look out at the countryside rather than talk.
   B He didn't speak to Guy because the driving conditions were difficult.
   C The fact that they travelled in silence seemed to make it longer.
   D It was much slower than usual because of the weather.

Writing | Part 1
An essay

Read this essay written by a student and the teacher's notes and then rewrite the essay, making the corrections that the teacher suggests.

Essay: Is it better to travel alone, or with other people?

In my opinion, travelling is very exciting, and <u>all people</u>, including me, likes to travel, because it ⟦is allowing⟧ you to <u>meet</u> new countries and cultures. But <u>that which</u> you have to decide is <u>if</u> you should travel alone, or with others. There are advantages and disadvantages to each. If you travel alone, you are free to ⟦going⟧ anywhere; there is no one who will <u>deny</u> to follow you to the place you want to go! However, you may feel extremely lonely. You haven't got anyone to enjoy the trip with. <u>Except</u> from that, a solo trip is more expensive, because you have to pay for everything yourself and you can't <u>divide</u> the cost with anyone. <u>In case</u> you travel with your friends, you will enjoy the journey more than if you are alone. Humans are social creatures and ⟦to be⟧ with someone else is good for your mind. With friends, the <u>travel</u> will not be boring! In fact, there aren't many disadvantages to travelling with friends. The only one is that you might ⟦be disagree⟧ with them about the places you want to visit. This isn't a serious disadvantage, because sooner or later you have to reach a decision. Finally, you could travel with your parents. This is the best <u>case</u> because you aren't responsible for anything and you go everywhere your parents go. You probably ⟦haven't⟧ to pay for anything yourself. However, if you are above the <u>years</u> of eighteen, you won't want to travel with your parents, because this <u>will</u> <u>guide</u> you, which is something you don't want. You ⟦must⟧ want to decide what to do and this is impossible with your parents around.

This is a good essay, but there are a few things you can do to improve it.

1 *In several places I've underlined where you've used the wrong word or expression, and you need to replace them with one of these words:*
   age, apart, discover, everyone, if, journey, refuse, restrict, share, solution, what, whether.

2 *I've shown six verbs where you've used the wrong form or tense.*

3 *Please divide your essay into four paragraphs!*

Our people

Listening | Part 4

▶ 02 You will hear five short extracts in which people are talking about their friends.

TASK ONE

For questions **1–5**, choose from the list (**A–H**) how each speaker originally met their friend.

TASK TWO

For questions **6–10**, choose from the list (**A–H**) the quality each speaker's friend has.

While you listen you must complete both tasks.

A at a musical event
B on public transport
C through a relative
D at school
E through another friend
F at work
G at a sporting event
H as a neighbour

Speaker 1 [1]
Speaker 2 [2]
Speaker 3 [3]
Speaker 4 [4]
Speaker 5 [5]

A a talent for listening
B a reluctance to criticise
C a desire to share
D willingness to apologise
E kindness to others
F enthusiasm for new ideas
G an ability to keep secrets
H continual optimism

Speaker 1 [6]
Speaker 2 [7]
Speaker 3 [8]
Speaker 4 [9]
Speaker 5 [10]

2 Mastering languages

Grammar
Expressing purpose, reason and result

1a Read this extract from a principal's letter and then complete the gaps with one of the phrases from the box below.

> due to   for this reason   in order not to   led to
> so as to   with the intention of   with the result that

Allerton Moor
High School

Dear Parent,

As you know, we have recently reduced the length of the school day and cut the length of breaks between lessons (1) ...so as to... maintain an orderly and purposeful movement of pupils around the premises.

I am pleased to report that, (2) .... the pupils' very positive response to the idea, the transition to the new timetable has been accomplished with the minimum of disruption. It has, in addition, (3) .... increased concentration levels, (4) .... most staff report a better learning environment. (5) .... I feel that the changes have been a complete success.

I would also like to emphasise that we introduced this shorter school day (6) .... offering a much wider choice of extracurricular activities, including sport and music. I am therefore delighted to report record enrolments for these activities. Finally, (7) .... disappoint a few students who we were unable to accommodate in the guitar class, we are now offering an additional class on Thursdays.

Yours faithfully,

Dr Tim Mortimer
Principal

b Read part of a dialogue between two friends and then complete the gaps with one of the phrases from the box below.

> because of   in case   make sure   means
> ~~otherwise~~   so

Well, I'd better go now, Anna, (1) ...otherwise... I'll be late for my music lesson. Shall I call you later (2) .... we can talk about where to meet up tomorrow?

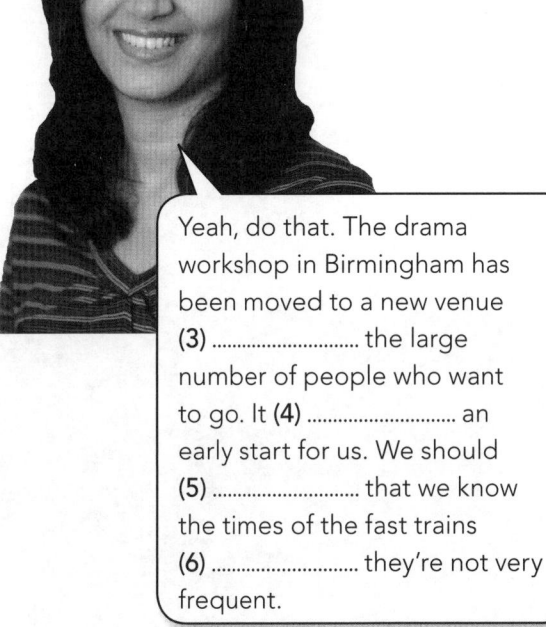

Yeah, do that. The drama workshop in Birmingham has been moved to a new venue (3) .... the large number of people who want to go. It (4) .... an early start for us. We should (5) .... that we know the times of the fast trains (6) .... they're not very frequent.

Mastering languages

Vocabulary
Expressions with *get*

1a Match the two halves of the sentence.

1 I told my sister how urgent the situation was,
2 Peter saw his boss to get some details straight
3 We've accepted the invitation for the party,
4 I'll get back to you
5 I had flu for three weeks
6 Once you've got into a difficult situation,
7 A teenage hacker managed
8 I'm always really nervous about interviews
9 We need to get a few basic things straight
10 Steve sent me a really lengthy email yesterday
11 Joe was determined to get into learning Japanese
12 Anna found the music at the party way too loud

a it's very hard to get out of it!
b and after a while it really got on her nerves.
c to get into the phone company records.
d but lack of time made him give it up.
e but I couldn't understand what he was getting at.
f before he finalised the report he was writing to her.
g so I'll have to get a grip on myself before I go in.
h but she didn't seem to get the point.
i as soon as I can answer your query.
j before we start working together.
k and it's great to get back to normal.
l so we can't get out of going to it now.

b Complete these sentences in your own words.

1 I often try to get out of ....
2 I'd never get into an argument about ....
3 I try to get out of difficult situations by ....
4 I usually get on well with ....

Word building

2a Write each of the suffixes below in the appropriate box.

-able -(u)al -ance -(e)n
-ence -ful -ical -ify
-(is)e -ity -ive -less -ment

b Now make words by adding one of the suffixes in 2a to the base words below. Put the new word in the correct circle.

broad centre class complex consider disappoint disturb
hard harm include instinct intuition maximum nation
occur progress purpose refer relevant responsible
scarce support thick

-able

Adjectives

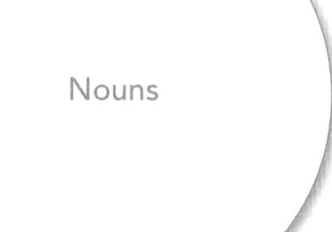
Nouns

Verbs

Writing | Part 2
A report

👁 Read the paragraphs A–E below, written by an exam candidate, and then put them into the correct order, using the linking phrases to help you. Decide on a heading for each paragraph. Then read each paragraph again and correct the spelling mistakes (there are 14 in total).

The correct order is:

1 .... 2 .... 3 .... 4 .... 5 ....

REPORT ON OUR ENGLISH LANGUAGE COURSE

A I also appreciated the fact that I was staying with a host family – it is a very good idea as there is more time for practising language. Unfortunetely, however, I lived some distance from the school and there were some unforeseen problems with the local transport. And one other comment I'd like to make is that what also needs improvment is the school cantean. There was remarkably little choice in what was on offer.

B On the whole, however, I must admit the course helped me develop my language skills and I lernt a lot of new language. I think, therefore, that in spite of some inconveniance such as transport or food problems, which are issues the college should address if possible, the course is very suitable for other trainees like me.

C In general, the course was well organised and the objectives fulfilled. What I appreciated most was the oportunity to improve my speaking skills. The teachers were very frendly and encouraged us to use the language and, as a result, the course gave me confidance. However, although I was pleased with my progress, in my opinion there could have been some more writing classes, as all of us needed these skills for our future use.

D Following your request I am submitting a report on the English course I attended in April this year. The aim of the course was to teach the participants English vocabulary as well as to develop and improve all our language skills.

E In addition, I think that the publisity about individual study was misleading. The study centre was poorly equipped, and the language laboratory frequently broke down, so you could hardly rely on them as aids for developing your listening skills. But what I did benefit from was a computer room with programes reinforcing the knowledge acquired during classes.

Reading and Use of English | Part 3

For questions **1–8**, read the text below. Use the word given in capitals at the end of some of the lines to form a word that fits in the gap in the same line. There is an example at the beginning (**0**).

Becoming an independent language learner

In an (**0**) ....*educational*.... context, the term 'learner independence' has gained increasing importance in recent years. It is of particular (**1**) .... to language learning. While some people seem to have an almost (**2**) .... flair for languages, there are in fact strategies that everyone can adopt to (**3**) .... their skills and learn a foreign language more (**4**) ....

EDUCATE

RELEVANT

INSTINCT

MAXIMUM

EFFECT

The main thing to remember is that becoming a truly independent learner ultimately depends above all on taking (**5**) .... for your own learning and being prepared to take every opportunity available to you to learn. You also increase your chances of success by learning according to your own needs and interests, using all available resources.

RESPONSIBLE

Research shows that learners who adopt this approach will (**6**) .... manage to (**7**) .... their language abilities considerably and as a result are more likely to achieve their (**8**) .... in the longer term.

DOUBT

BROAD

OBJECT

Mastering languages

Reading and Use of English | Part 4

For questions **1–6**, complete the second sentence so that it has a similar meaning to the first sentence, using the word given. **Do not change the word given**. You must use between **three** and **six** words, including the word given. Here is an example (**0**).

Example:

0 I've never been at all interested in learning to play a musical instrument.
   SLIGHTEST
   I've never ......*had the slightest interest in*...... learning to play a musical instrument.

1 Susan picked the baby up gently, because she didn't want to wake him.
   TO
   Susan picked the baby up gently so .... him.

2 They were able to creep away unobserved because it was very dark.
   OWING
   They were able to creep away unobserved .... it was very dark.

3 The car was redesigned and, as a result, sales rose rapidly.
   RESULTED
   The successful redesigning of the car .... in sales.

4 Despite improving his performance, Smith is still not in the top three for the 10,000 metres.
   LED
   The improvement in Smith's performance .... in the top three for the 10,000 metres.

5 You should make the sauce thicker if you want to improve the flavour.
   THICKEN
   You'll .... order to improve the flavour.

6 After several years, heavy traffic caused the bridge to collapse.
   DUE
   The collapse .... several years of heavy traffic.

Listening | Part 3

▶ 03 You will hear an interview in which an Irish-Australian writer called Patrick O'Reilly is talking about the Irish-Gaelic language. For questions **1–6**, choose the answer (**A**, **B**, **C** or **D**) which fits best according to what you hear.

1 Why is the Irish language significant to Patrick?
   A It was spoken to him when he was a child.
   B It evokes city life in a particular era.
   C It came close to disappearing at one time.
   D It is a major part of his cultural heritage.

2 Which aspect of Irish has particularly impressed Patrick?
   A its age as a language
   B its suitability for song lyrics
   C its success in the modern world
   D its role in broadcasting

3 Why was Patrick keen to learn Irish?
   A He lacked a strong identity as an Australian.
   B He was reacting against other people's views.
   C He was aware that it would broaden his horizons.
   D He wanted to be actively involved in its revival.

4 According to Patrick, what makes Irish different from other languages in Australia?
   A It is impossible to show how it sounds.
   B It is not a language published in Australia.
   C It is used as a second language.
   D It has not gone through a process of evolution.

5 What reason does Patrick give for Irish becoming fashionable?
   A Speaking languages fluently has become a status symbol.
   B It is associated with the popularity of the country.
   C It is seen as the language of well-known fairy tales.
   D Many Irish-Australians now aspire to live in Ireland.

6 What does Patrick say about other people's explanations of why they are learning Irish?
   A They may not reveal the whole truth.
   B They show they are trying to reassure themselves.
   C They reveal a lack of self-awareness.
   D They indicate that people feel little need to justify themselves.

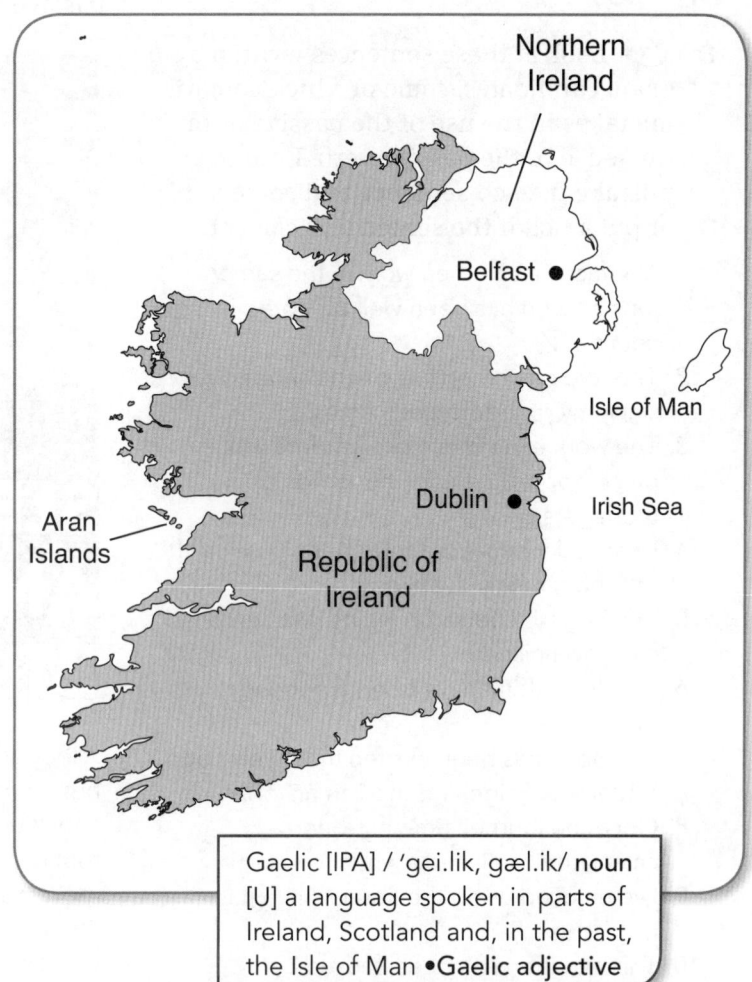

Gaelic [IPA] / ˈgeɪ.lɪk, gæl.ɪk/ noun [U] a language spoken in parts of Ireland, Scotland and, in the past, the Isle of Man •Gaelic adjective

3 All in the mind

Grammar
The passive

1a 👁 Look at these sentences written by exam candidates, some of which contain mistakes in the use of the passive or in the tense of the passive verb. Find the mistake in each sentence and correct it or put a tick if the sentence is correct.

1 The fact that women work in the same jobs as men has been well accepted in my country. ✓
2 The role of women has been changed a lot since my grandmother's times.
3 The work experience programme was given opportunities to hundreds of teenagers.
4 I was lucky because I have been given a lift to school nearly every day.
5 The English course on which I was enrolled has now finished.
6 I really couldn't have been agreed with you more.
7 The book has been written three years ago by Jemma Paige, a Canadian historian.
8 Once the journey time has been calculated, we'll know when to set off.
9 I've enjoyed using the library since it is modernised.
10 This situation has been caused by negligence.
11 I was looking forward to the trip but it has been suddenly cancelled yesterday.
12 Our company will definitely be benefited from the new invention.
13 Mount Jiree has been thought to be thousands of years old, but no one is sure.
14 Shops can have been found at only 200 metres from the apartment.
15 If I studied harder, my work might be improved more.

b Look at sentences 1–15 again and decide which of the incorrect sentences:

- had passive verbs in the wrong tense?
  ....
- needed an active verb not a passive one?
  ....

2 Read this extract from an article and then put the words in brackets into the correct order, using the appropriate form of the passive.

SLEEP AND DREAMS

Although they have been a topic of speculation throughout human history, the content and purpose of dreams **(1)** _are not understood_ (not / understand). It **(2)** .... (now / acknowledge) that dreams **(3)** .... (strongly / link) to the rapid eye movement that takes place during the first stage of sleep. Over the full course of a typical human lifespan, a total approaching six years may **(4)** .... (spend) dreaming. Yet, despite this, it **(5)** .... (not / establish) where in the brain dreams originate, or whether they have a common cause.

Philosophers and artists **(6)** .... (for centuries / fascinate) by sleep and dreams. Yet they **(7)** .... (often / portray) as a dark and often disturbing sphere of human existence, despite the fact that it **(8)** .... (know / for many years) that both physical survival and mental wellbeing depend upon them.

Two thousand years ago, dreams **(9)** .... (regularly / interpret) as supernatural or divine communication, and they **(10)** .... (therefore / think) to foretell the future. By the beginning of the twentieth century, the interpretation of dreams **(11)** .... (most commonly / associate) with psychoanalysis and its famous practitioners, Freud and Jung, who regarded dreams as the bridge between the unconscious and conscious mind, a tool with which the secrets of the human mind could **(12)** .... (finally / unlock). But the key to those secrets has **(13)** .... (yet / find).

Vocabulary

Nouns which can be countable or uncountable

1 Use one of the nouns in the sentences below, and mark whether their use is countable (C) or uncountable (U).

> appetite   cancellation   escape   pressure
> reference   suspicion

1 The dentist said he had a ...*cancellation*... that afternoon, so he was able to see me at 3.00.
   (Countable)/ Uncountable

2 These days many employees find themselves under constant .... at work.
   Countable / Uncountable

3 The article stated that James King was arrested yesterday on .... of murder.
   Countable / Uncountable

4 A lot of novels are based on the theme of .... from the monotony of everyday life.
   Countable / Uncountable

5 Thirty years had passed, and Peter consequently no longer had any .... for revenge.
   Countable / Uncountable

6 I heard a .... to the traffic incident on the news that day.
   Countable / Uncountable

7 I had a strong .... that my sister had borrowed my black shoes without asking.
   Countable / Uncountable

8 The .... in my tyres was low so I pumped them up before I started the journey.
   Countable / Uncountable

9 My cat had a narrow .... this morning when it ran out in front of a car.
   Countable / Uncountable

10 We should keep that guidebook of Paris for future .... as we'll be going back soon.
   Countable / Uncountable

11 Within 14 days of your holiday, ... will incur loss of all booking fees.
   Countable / Uncountable

12 My brother has an absolutely huge .... and eats twice what I do.
   Countable / Uncountable

Word building

2 1 Make the abstract nouns formed from these base words.

> able   apt   critic   evolve   recognise
> *recognition*   relation

2 Name the people associated with these nouns.

> archaeology   *architect*   architecture   education
> novel   paint   surgery

3 Make the adjective(s) formed from these nouns.

> analysis   courage   decision   mind   *mindless*
> philosophy   point   skill

4 Make the adverbs formed from these base words.

> character   critic   *critically*   increase   nature
> psychology   science

3 Use an appropriate form of one of these words to complete 1–8.

> analyse   apt   ~~character~~   critic   decide   increase
> point   science

1 As soon as I heard Sarah's ...*characteristic*... laugh, I knew she was somewhere in the crowd.

2 .... speaking, the project was extremely sound.

3 Much to the relief of the staff, it seems .... unlikely that the company will be taken over.

4 Opting to go to university was definitely a .... moment in my life.

5 Not everyone has the appropriate .... for becoming a pilot.

6 Some students find it difficult to accept constructive .... of the work they do.

7 It's often .... to argue with someone once they have made up their mind about something.

8 Peter has a very .... mind, so I think he'll make a very good researcher.

All in the mind

Writing | Part 1
An essay

Read this advanced student's essay and divide it into four paragraphs. Rewrite it, replacing the words and phrases in italics with one of the more formal expressions in box A. You should also replace the verbs underlined with one of the more formal verbs in box B.

A

> almost certainly assured   an alternative   despite following this advice
> finally   find the workload manageable   firstly   however
> in addition   in my opinion   in your own mind
> one method of doing this   purely   the teaching methods
> ~~there is no doubt that~~   ultimately prove disastrous

B

> analyse   establish   ~~gather~~   inquire   locate   require   transfer

Methods students should adopt to select the right university

There is no doubt that
~~I'm sure that~~ choosing what to study at university is one of the biggest decisions you will ever make in your life. This is because if you make the right choice, a successful future is *probably guaranteed*. *But* making the wrong one can *be a catastrophe at the end of the day*. So how can you ensure success? *To start with*, I believe you should ~~get~~ *(gather)* as much information as possible. *A good way* is to talk to people who are already attending the course you are interested in, to find out what their experience of it has been. Ask about *how it's taught* and whether they benefit from the lectures and seminars. Check how many contact hours they have per week, and whether they *can cope with all the work they get*. *Another thing you can do* is to go online; you can also find the information you need in forums and chat rooms. *And,* examine *what you yourself think* about whether you are doing it *just* for interest and enjoyment, or to qualify for a career. *So,* if *after you've done what I suggested* you are still unfortunate enough to find you've made the wrong decision, *I think* the best thing you can do is to talk to your tutors and find out whether it is possible to move to another course.

Reading and Use of English | Part 6

You are going to read four reviews of a psychology book. For questions **1–4**, choose from the reviews **A–D**. The reviews may be chosen more than once.

Smart Thinking

Four reviewers comment on psychology professor Art Markman's book called *Smart Thinking*.

A
For anyone needing to learn more about the mind and how it works, I'd recommend *Smart Thinking*. This book explains how we can ingest valuable information and then become more adept at retaining and recalling it, becoming better thinkers as a result. That's an appealing idea. Markman is clearly an expert in his field, but he doesn't flash data in a way that leaves the reader befuddled and confused. He writes in such a way that seemingly complex concepts are perceptively unravelled, and the workings of the human mind are laid bare. Although not every chapter is a winner, the whole book is filled with practical ideas anyone can use which are based on the principles of sound scientific research. It is an excellent read, and well worth perusing in detail for its insights.

B
Smart Thinking is a fascinating book for those whose goal is to retain more useful information. It combines common-sense advice with the author's experience in the field of cognitive psychology. While not every point is helpful, there is much to like. Markman wants us to understand that we use mental energy in much the same way as we consume physical energy. When we are in our comfort zones, working with familiar subjects, thinking comes easily. So, he posits, our goal should be to make more subjects familiar ones. For instance, are you able to move about a room in the dark? If so, that's because you have made it a habit to manuever around objects by making a connection between an action (your movement) and an environment (the room). When we make that connection in other learning situations such as a classroom or meeting room, it assists the brain with the retaining of information.

C
Smart Thinking by Art Markman is based on leading-edge science, but targeted at the lay reader. Its stated aim is to reach into the underlying ability to reason, make decisions, communicate, and take action. It strives to do this by presenting innate, intuitive human ability in a structured 'how to' layout, thus implying the things that make people different are a matter of learning a new skill. Markman consequently implies for instance, that with training anyone can invent an ingenious device. But the reader may have reservations about the information that Markman tries to instill in his narrative, principally because there is no overt acknowledgement that imagination, the motor of intelligence, can rarely be duplicated by training. All in all, this book does little to define motivation or imagination, yet its subject matter alone could well ensure its success.

D
Because *Smart Thinking* is marketed primarily as a self-help book, potential readers might overlook the fact that this is an excellent treatise on cognitive psychology. In fact, Markman is one of the best in the business at synthesizing what cognitive psychologists have learned about how the mind works. There is some innovative content and the reader cannot fail to appreciate with just what lucidity and intelligence Markman expounds on and applies various concepts. Many of his examples, and the logic with which he lays out various principles, are better executed than formal psychology lectures normally are. For those who aren't as versed in cognitive science literature, this will be a ground-breaking read full of useful practical tips, and for others who are already expert, there is still much of value in this carefully constructed tome.

Which reviewer

1 shares reviewer A's view that Markham has a gift for communicating clearly?
2 has a different opinion from the others on the immediate relevance of Markham's ideas to daily life?
3 makes a comparison similar to that of reviewer B of the effective and ineffective elements of Markham's discussion?
4 has a different view to reviewer C on the appeal of the book to professionals in the field?

All in the mind

Listening | Part 1

▶ 04 You will hear three different extracts. For questions **1–6**, choose the answer (**A**, **B** or **C**) which fits best according to what you hear. There are two questions for each extract.

Extract One

You hear two friends talking about an incident one of them has seen.

1 What happened to the woman's car?
   A It was slightly scratched when a lorry reversed.
   B It was completely destroyed when a lorry drove over it.
   C It escaped damage when a lorry turned round.

2 How did the woman react to what had happened?
   A She was disappointed about missing her day out.
   B She felt some sympathy for the lorry driver.
   C She was extremely angry with the lorry driver.

Extract Two

On the radio, you hear a zoo director talking about the orang-utans at the zoo.

3 How did visitors at the zoo react to Marla's escape?
   A They were curious and crowded round to watch Marla.
   B They were worried about Marla and offered her food.
   C They were frightened because Marla seemed threatening.

4 Which of Marla's actions does the zoo director find particularly clever?
   A managing to hide some keys
   B using sign cards in an appropriate way
   C understanding why the vet had arrived

Extract Three

On the radio, you hear two people talking about a stonemason.

5 What was the stonemason's initial response to the people around him?
   A He felt stopping work to speak to them was a waste of time.
   B He seemed to be completely unaware of their presence.
   C He was very willing to describe his skills and techniques.

6 Why were the onlookers so fascinated by the stonemason's work?
   A They believed his work had made him famous.
   B They valued craft work because it had become fashionable.
   C They found the idea of practical work appealing.

4 Just the job!

Grammar
Expressing possibility, probability and certainty

1 Choose the correct modal verb in each sentence.

1. When you choose a book for a child to read, it *can't* / *shouldn't* be too difficult for their age.
2. Katerina knew it *can't* / *couldn't* be Igor ringing the doorbell because he had a key.
3. When the new students arrived, there was nobody to welcome them and this *mustn't* / *shouldn't* have happened.
4. If you give Angelo the news now it *could* / *must* upset him, so tell him later on.
5. Jack isn't here yet so he *must* / *should* be waiting for Rose who's always late.
6. According to the directions, the hotel *could* / *should* have been next to the park but there was only a garage there.
7. If we offer free sandwiches, it *can* / *may* encourage more people to attend the lecture.
8. We are looking for people who *might* / *should* be able to write reviews for the magazine.

2 ▶05 Read what a student said about the photographs of the two jobs below and choose the correct word. Then listen and check your answers.

The people in the first photo are working in a lab. They **(1)** *may* / *can* be students in a university or it **(2)** *could* / *must* be a hospital but it's difficult to tell. It seems highly likely that they're doing some kind of research though. They **(3)** *could* / *can* be working separately but it is more **(4)** *possible* / *likely* that they are working together with the man taking notes. There's a **(5)** *strong* / *little* likelihood that they are working with chemicals as the woman has protective glasses on. This kind of work demands a high level of accuracy and **(6)** *must* / *can't* be very rewarding if you're good at it. In the second photo the people are doing a tour of a famous place. They **(7)** *must* / *can* have travelled to the place together with a tour guide. She **(8)** *can* / *might* be telling them about the history of the area as she has something in her hand. She looks interested in what she's saying even though she **(9)** *might* / *should* have said the same thing lots of times before. It looks quite cold as everyone is wearing coats but it **(10)** *must* / *might* well be summer in some northern European country!'

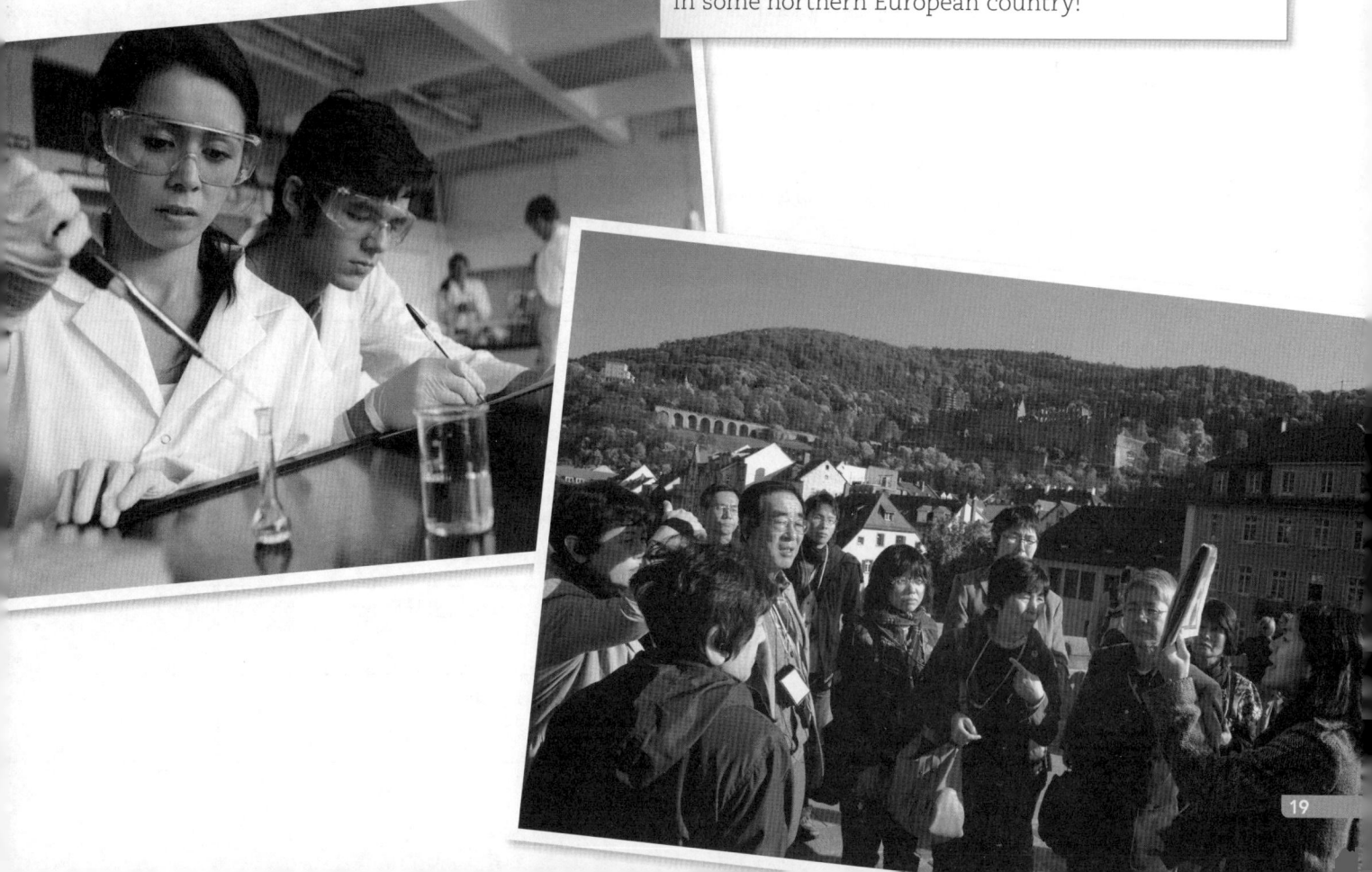

Just the job!

Vocabulary
Adjective–noun collocations

1a For each group of four, match the word on the left to a word on the right to make a suitable collocation.

flexible	leave
employment	working conditions
poor	agency
sick	working hours

minimum	balance
work/life	responsibility
temporary	contract
managerial	wage

foolproof	pressure
major	solution
constant	workload
heavy	drawback

b Put one of the expressions above in each space.

I'm an architect. I started in my company at the age of 25 when I was on a (1) ...temporary contract... and earning the (2) .... Since then, I've worked my way up and I've now got (3) .... for several of our major projects and ten members of staff. I love my job but there is one (4) .... which is the fact that I have a very (5) .... and I'm under (6) .... to make sure we meet all our deadlines. The great thing is that if I work a lot of extra hours I can take a day off as we have (7) .... , so if you are a really good organiser you can have a good (8) .... and make time for leisure when you want it.

work and job

2 Complete the sentences, using *work* or *job*.

1 I like outdoor ....work.......... so I'm applying for a job as a tour guide.
2 If you want to get a .... in a big company, you'll probably have to attend several interviews.
3 As people climb the promotion ladder, they tend to spend longer and longer at .... as their responsibilities increase.
4 I really like living in Sydney so I'm planning to find .... here.
5 I'm going to do a full-time course so I'm leaving my .... at the health club at the end of the week.
6 I'd like to accept the .... of deputy manager offered to me in your email received yesterday.

Dependent prepositions

3 👁 Look at these sentences written by exam candidates. Correct the underlined prepositions.

1 The newspaper devoted a whole column <u>for</u> the charity event. (to)
2 I was pleased to participate <u>at</u> the discussion about the future of the sports club.
3 I hope you will find the proposal adequate <u>to</u> your needs.
4 The additional investment <u>to</u> advertising resulted in increased company profits.
5 The school has a reputation <u>of</u> producing winning athletes.
6 There has been a gradual decline <u>of</u> the number of new members.
7 Carlos never seems to be at a loss <u>of</u> words.
8 The employees were rewarded with an increase <u>of</u> their salary of 6 per cent.
9 My manager is very sensitive <u>for</u> other people's needs.
10 Over the last fifty years, many changes <u>of</u> working conditions have taken place.

Word building

4a Make adverbs from these adjectives. There is one adjective that does not change.

actual ......ly......	basic	common ....
extraordinary	fast	full ....
general	historic	incredible ....
private	public	realistic ....
satisfactory	shy	sincere ....
suitable	true	whole ....

b Write the adverbs in the correct place in the table. Think of one more adverb to add to each line.

To make an adverb:	
add *-ly* to adjective:	*actually*
change *-y* at end of adjective to *-i* and add *-ly*:	
change *-le* at end of adjective after a consonant to *-ly*:	
add *-ally* to adjective:	
Exceptions:	

Reading and Use of English | Part 3

For questions 1–10, read the text below. Use the word given in capitals at the end of some of the lines to form a word that fits in the gap in the same line. There is an example at the beginning (0).

Putting some fun into the workplace

In a study of 737 chief executives working in large corporations, the vast (0) ......*majority*...... gave the same answer **MAJOR**
when asked what kind of person they like to employ. Ninety-eight per cent said they would hire someone with a cheerful attitude, (1) .... with a good sense **PREFER**
of humour.
Having fun at work apparently inspires (2) .... in employees. A survey of **LOYAL**
1,000 workers showed how (3) .... **SIGNIFY**
their manager's sense of humour or lack of it was to the (4) .... of time they **LONG**
stayed in a job. If they worked for a boss whose sense of humour they described as 'below average', the employee's (5) .... of staying dropped to **LIKELY**
seventy-seven per cent compared to ninety per cent for a boss who had an 'above average' sense of humour.
Laughter may be both (6) .... **BENEFIT**
and good for business but it isn't (7) .... a positive aspect of **NECESSARY**
all jobs. Some people working in retail jobs are required to smile continuously. Such enforced happiness can cause (8) .... at work and also result in **SATISFY**
emotional stress.

Writing | Part 2
A report

◉ Read this report written by an exam candidate. First, choose the most suitable formal expression and then write a suitable heading for each of the paragraphs, A–E.

Report to the Principal on changes to catering arrangements in the college canteen

A Introduction
The aim of this report is to (1) *give* / *point out* the advantages and disadvantages of the two catering companies we are considering to manage our canteen. Students have been complaining about (2) *not having* / *the lack of* healthy food and limited opening hours, so I have carefully (3) *examined* / *looked at* what each company is offering in relation to this.

B ....
Kavanagh Catering Services (KCS) (4) *talk about offering* / *propose to offer* fast food and snacks (5) *throughout the day* / *all day*, but (6) *they don't say* / *there is no mention of* how healthy these snacks are. In contrast, Rainbow Ltd (RL) (7) *emphasise* / *say* that their meals are all made from fresh ingredients and that they will offer nutritious food and also herbal teas.

C ....
Students eat at the college five times a week so a varied menu is (8) *crucial* / *needed*. KCS offer fast food and snacks and some hot meals, but they don't (9) *state* / *say* how often their menu changes. RL offer hot meals and salads. Their menu changes daily, they have a choice of two special hot dishes a day but (10) *it doesn't look like they* / *they don't appear to* include many salads.

D ....
KCS (11) *guarantee* / *promise* to stay open from 8 am to 10 pm. However, they will not serve hot food of any kind after 6 pm. RL are only open from 9 am to 6 pm, and they only serve hot meals for a (12) *short* / *limited* time from 12 to 2.

E ....
I suggest that we (13) *accept* / *agree to* the contract with RL even though they only serve hot meals from 12 to 2. Whilst it is not possible for students to eat a full meal outside these times, RL still offers snack food during the (14) *remainder* / *rest* of the day, and in addition they will provide a variety of food. I am certain that the majority of our students will be happy with this arrangement as it addresses both issues related to the current unsatisfactory provision.

Reading and Use of English | Part 4

For questions **1–6**, complete the second sentence so that it has a similar meaning to the first sentence, using the word given. **Do not change the word given**. You must use between **three** and **six** words, including the word given. Here is an example (**0**).

Example:

0 I gave up the job at the hotel because there were too few challenges.

   ENOUGH

   I gave up the job at the hotel because it ....*wasn't challenging enough*........ for me.

1 There is a strong possibility that the manager will choose Antonio to play on Saturday but it depends on his state of fitness.

   WELL

   Antonio .... the manager to play on Saturday but it depends on his state of fitness.

2 We are sure that the government's new policy will successfully reduce unemployment.

   BOUND

   We think that the government's new policy .... in reducing unemployment.

3 You can't blame Sam for breaking the window because he wasn't even here this morning.

   BEEN

   It .... broke the window because he wasn't even here this morning.

4 It is not likely that the effects of global warming can be reversed.

   LIKELIHOOD

   There is .... reversing the effects of global warming.

5 Some people tend to do better in a pressurised working environment.

   CONSTANT

   Some people work better when they are .... work.

6 I do not intend to stay in my present job very much longer.

   NO

   I have .... in my present job very much longer.

Listening | Part 4

▶ 06 You will hear five short extracts in which people are talking about their jobs.

TASK ONE
For questions **1–5**, choose from the list (**A–H**) each speaker's job.

TASK TWO
For questions **6–10**, choose from the list (**A–H**) what each speaker says they enjoy most about their job.

While you listen you must complete both tasks.

A air traffic controller
B engineer
C fashion buyer
D interior designer
E museum director
F shop assistant
G lawyer
H website designer

Speaker 1 [1]
Speaker 2 [2]
Speaker 3 [3]
Speaker 4 [4]
Speaker 5 [5]

A extending existing skills
B doing accounts
C keeping regular hours
D managing staff
E meeting new people
F satisfying customers
G travelling abroad
H working as a team

Speaker 1 [6]
Speaker 2 [7]
Speaker 3 [8]
Speaker 4 [9]
Speaker 5 [10]

5 Dramatic events

Grammar
Verbs followed by *to* + infinitive or the *ing* form

1 Read this extract from a biography and then complete the gaps with an infinitive or verb + *-ing* form, using the verb in brackets.

Ranulph Fiennes is a man who isn't afraid of (1) ...pushing... (*push*) himself to the limits. He's famous for (2) .... (*visit*) both the North and South Poles by land between 1979 and 1982 and (3) .... (*cross*) the Antarctic on foot in 1993.

In 2000 he attempted (4) .... (*reach*) the North Pole on his own at the age of 55. On that trip, there was too much food and equipment for a single sledge (5) .... (*transport*), so he took two. This meant (6) .... (*walk*) one mile forward with the first sledge, then (7) .... (*go*) back for the second one so every mile gained involved (8) .... (*travel*) three on the ground. To do such a trip with one sledge is dangerous enough, but it is much worse with two. After (9) .... (*park*) the first sledge, you then have to set off (10) .... (*fetch*) the second one but if conditions get worse, however hard you try (11) .... (*find*) it, you may never see it again. Fiennes didn't ever lose his sledges in the snow but at one point during the journey, they fell through weak ice and he was forced (12) .... (*pull*) them out by hand. He would have kept (13) .... (*go*) but he got frostbite in his fingers which made it impossible for him (14) .... (*carry on*).

The experiences Fiennes had that time discouraged him from (15) .... (*make*) another attempt but he was not ready to stop (16) .... (*push*) himself to the limits. Since then he has carried out the extraordinary feat of (17) .... (*complete*) seven marathons in seven days on seven continents and in 2009 succeeded in (18) .... (*reach*) the summit of Everest at the age of 65.

2 Read each pair of sentences and then answer the question which follows.

1 A I forgot to take change for the bus fare.
  B I'll never forget going in an aeroplane for the first time.
  In which sentence did the speaker fail to do something? ......A......

2 A Jessie didn't stop complaining about her legs aching until she saw the view from the top of the hill.
  B When we'd walked halfway up the hill, I stopped to admire the view.
  In which sentence did someone stop for a purpose? ....

3 A I tried to tell Simon but I just couldn't.
  B I tried sailing but I didn't like it.
  In which sentence did someone attempt something difficult? ....

4 A The woman who used to live in the basement below us went on to become a famous writer.
  B My uncle went on playing professional football until he was nearly 40.
  In which sentence did something continue for a period of time? ....

5 A The college regrets to inform students that their results will be delayed by a week.
  B The students regret not paying more attention during classes.
  Which sentence is looking back at something that has already happened? ....

6 A They'd meant to travel by coach but it was already full when they got to the coach station.
  B Travelling by plane means allowing plenty of time to get to the airport.
  Which sentence refers to an intention? ....

7 A Everyone applauded loudly when they heard Peter sing his solo.
  B We heard Peter rehearsing his solo when we arrived at the hall.
  In which sentence did someone hear only part of Peter's solo? ....

Vocabulary
Useful words and expressions

1 Complete this crossword puzzle.

Across

3 My brother loves arguing and he's always picking a .... with me over nothing.
4 I put my foot down on the .... in order to overtake the lorry.
5 Time stood .... while we waited to be rescued from the mountain.
7 I find using the .... in the gym much more enjoyable than jogging.
9 Can you keep an .... on that sauce for me while I make a phone call.
10 Shona has been really ill with food poisoning but she's on the .... now.

Down

1 You can build up your .... by jogging a bit further every day.
2 You have to have nerves of .... to be a driving instructor.
3 I kept on having .... to the day when I went sailing and got caught in a terrible storm.
5 As soon as we'd packed our bags, we .... up and left the hotel.
6 I remember slipping on a rock but everything's a bit of a .... after that.
8 A deer ran in front of the car and as I braked desperately, everything seemed to go into slow ....

Writing | Part 2
A proposal

Read this proposal written by an exam candidate. Then replace the underlined words, using one of the words or phrases from the box below to improve the vocabulary level and make the proposal more formal.

> a wide range of   appreciate   as well as   assistance
> compose   declined   donate   forthcoming events
> had in mind   personalities   professional responsibilities
> scheduled   such as   taking into consideration
> ~~the contents of~~

Sports and Social Club proposal: publishing a magazine for members

This proposal to the committee includes some ideas about *the contents of* (1) <u>what is in</u> the first edition. (2) <u>Thinking about</u> the secretary's suggestions (3) <u>and</u> some ideas from other committee members, I believe that the first edition should contain (4) <u>different</u> subjects to attract the interest of all its readers.

First of all we could include interviews with famous sports (5) <u>people</u> like Gerry Armstrong, the Scottish footballer. I also (6) <u>thought of</u> Joe Hill, the tennis player, but unfortunately he (7) <u>did not accept</u> my invitation due to his (8) <u>job</u>. However, he offered to (9) <u>give</u> one of his tennis racquets as a competition prize in our magazine.

Secondly, considering that our readers (10) <u>like</u> receiving advice on keeping fit, I arranged with Ken Brown, the sports centre instructor, to (11) <u>write</u> an article including his ideas and instructions on how our athletes can improve their fitness levels. To make the magazine entertaining, I suggest we should include competitions, (12) <u>like</u> sports crosswords, and also film and book reviews. Also, there should be announcements about (13) <u>what's happening soon</u> at our Club, such as the party and barbecue for our members, which are (14) <u>planned</u> for next month. Finally, I suggest that we should recommend the top restaurants in our town.

I hope that the above suggestions will be of (15) <u>help</u> to the committee for the first edition of our magazine.

Reading and Use of English | Part 7

You are going to read an extract from an article about a sport. Six paragraphs have been removed from the extract. Choose from the paragraphs **A–G** the one which fits each gap (**1–6**). There is one extra paragraph which you do not need to use.

The scariest ride on the planet

Charles Starmer-Smith spent a weekend in Norway learning how to ride on a bob skeleton, a one-person sledge which races down an ice track at 60 mph.

I glanced down at the red snow by my feet just a few yards from the finishing gate of the Lillehammer bob skeleton track. The bob skeleton is also known as a toboggan and reminded me of a tray a waiter might use to bring plates of food out in a restaurant. But this one was going to have me on it rather than a pile of food so seeing the blood of an earlier rider was a little unnerving. Make no bones about it, this has to be one of the scariest rides on the planet.

| 1 |

I feigned nonchalance at this information, but I was fooling no one. I have made a habit of scaring myself: I've leapt down the face of Switzerland's Verzasca Dam – the world's biggest bungee jump, I have descended the near-vertical Corbets Couloir at Jacksonhole – perhaps the most fearsome ski run in North America – and I have learnt to ski-jump at Calgary.

| 2 |

At least I was not alone as several other novices would be joining me. After a fitful sleep, we went out early to walk to the top of the track. The snow, hanging heavy on the branches of Lillehammer's forested slopes, made the track look even more imposing. Snaking down the slope like a giant metallic python, the walls were steeper, the straights were longer but the 16 turns were much sharper than I expected.

| 3 |

Halfway up, we arrived at the infamous Turn 13, a shuddering 180-degree U-turn where the centrifugal pressures equal those experienced by fighter pilots. 'This is where you'll feel the full force,' said Tony, our instructor, his eyes sparkling. 'So, is the track running quickly?' I asked tentatively. He did not need to answer.

| 4 |

All we caught was a flash of eyeballs and overalls as the rider sliced around the curved wall of ice at breathtaking speed. We glanced at each other, panic etched across our faces and laughed the nervous laugh of the truly terrified as we realised this would soon be us.

| 5 |

I therefore took comfort in the knowledge that, with a professional in charge, someone would be keeping his head while the rest of us were losing ours. I drew the short straw and was given position four, where you feel the full brunt of the force with nothing but cool Norwegian air behind you.

| 6 |

We barely had time to check that we were all in one piece before we were sent off to get kitted up for the skeleton. On Tony's instructions I lay face down on the sledge, arms clamped by my sides, nose inches from the ice and off I went. After seventy seconds of terror, I could barely speak and my body felt as though it had been in a boxing ring, but I had never felt so alive. What a ride!

A Before we had any more time to contemplate our fate, we found ourselves at the top, climbing aboard a bobraft. Designed to give you a feel for the track before going down on your own, this giant, padded open-top box looked about as aerodynamic as a bus, but it travelled a whole lot faster. It had a driver who did this all the time which was reassuring.

B As if on cue, snow crystals began to jump in unison on the metallic railings as, high above, a sledge began its inexorable journey down. What started as a distant hum became a rattle, then a roar as the sledge reached top speed. The tarpaulin covering the track stiffened in its wake and the girders groaned.

C On these previous occasions, I had had experience or the expertise of others to fall back on, but with this there was nothing from which to draw strength. The bob skeleton confounds conventional logic.

D It started deceptively slowly, but within moments picked up speed. It soon became clear that the rider has little control and survival instinct takes over.

E It is hard to describe the debilitating effect that such immense speeds and forces have on your body. It was like nothing I have ever experienced. The last thing I remember going through my mind was straining just to keep my head upright.

F We listened to advice on how to get round them safely – use your eyes to steer and tilt your head away from the corners to minimise the pressure. It sounded simple enough, but get it wrong at these speeds and your chin faces the cheese-grater.

G The man behind these adrenalin-packed weekends at Norway's Olympic park, explained that those who attempt the famous run often accidentally 'kiss' the ice with their nose or chin, leaving a layer or three of skin behind.

Dramatic events

Listening | Part 3

▶ 07 You will hear an interview in which two people called Sarah and Peter who work in air and sea rescue are talking about their work. For questions **1–6**, choose the answer (**A**, **B**, **C** or **D**) which fits best according to what you hear.

1 What do Sarah and Peter agree is most important when working in sea rescue?
 A a lack of anxiety in unknown situations
 B a willingness to follow instructions
 C a certain amount of specialised knowledge
 D an ability to get along with colleagues

2 Peter says the main difficulty in a rescue operation is
 A lack of appropriate equipment.
 B shortage of time.
 C unpredictable weather.
 D lengthy journeys.

3 Sarah criticises the people they rescued last week because they
 A miscalculated how long their journey would take.
 B underestimated the distance they faced.
 C paid little attention to the weather forecast.
 D began their journey in unfavourable conditions.

4 What does Peter say is the disadvantage of using a helicopter in a rescue?
 A It is hard to keep in one position.
 B It makes communication difficult.
 C It cannot land on dangerous rocks.
 D It gets very cold inside it.

5 Sarah gets annoyed when people being rescued
 A are not grateful enough.
 B have the wrong priorities.
 C panic unnecessarily.
 D refuse assistance.

6 What does Peter say he plans to do next?
 A pass on his knowledge to others
 B apply for a less hazardous position
 C get promoted to a better job
 D use his skills in different circumstances

28

6 Picture yourself

Grammar
Avoiding repetition

Read this book review of *The Thirteenth Tale* and then complete the gaps, using the reference words from the box.

all	both	during which	~~first~~	following	what	for herself	her own
herself	including	it is	through	living there	neither	none
of her own	one of	these	this	which	whose	

REVIEW

The Thirteenth Tale by Diane Setterfield

This gripping novel, Diane Setterfield's (1) ...first..., could best be described as a mystery story. Margaret Lee, a young biographer, is summoned by Vida Winter, a novelist of considerable renown, to write her biography. It is (2) .... sets Margaret on a voyage of discovery, not only about Vida's life, but about (3) .... life too.

Vida has led a secretive and reclusive life, (4) .... she has created many outlandish life histories (5) ...., all of them pure fantasy. It is only as she comes to the end of her life that she feels able to expose the secrets of her past. Margaret travels to Vida's home in Yorkshire, (6) .... with Vida while she writes the biography. As a biographer, Margaret deals in fact not fiction, so as Vida tells her story, Margaret embarks on research (7) .... to establish the truth. (8) .... the coming together of (9) .... two accounts that the reader gradually discovers how the eminent author has kept the family secrets and made a success of her life (10) .... can only be described as a very disturbed childhood.

Vida's tale is (11) .... gothic strangeness featuring the Angelfield family, headed by the beautiful but unstable Isabelle. Her twin daughters, (12) .... bizarre behaviour brings havoc to those around them, are called Adeline and Emmeline. It soon becomes apparent from the twins' behaviour that (13) .... is capable of leading a normal life, and when the house they live in is deliberately set alight one night, it seems at first that (14) .... the girls have perished in the fire.

As Margaret gradually unravels the truth about Vida, it becomes apparent that (15) .... of the people involved with the twins, (16) .... the housekeeper and the gardener, escaped unscathed, so the story is to a large extent one of tragedy. But by the end of the novel, (17) .... is resolved and even the smallest of details in Vida's story has its place. Meanwhile, there is a hint that Margaret (18) .... is about to find a happy ending.

Vocabulary
Adjective–noun collocations

1a Match an adjective in column A to a noun in column B. Use each adjective only once.

A	B
deafening	clothing
fashionable	criticism
gripping	exuberance
harsh	experience
hazardous	~~feedback~~
innate	honesty
~~instant~~	journey
sheer	noise
total	story
wide	talent

b Complete the gaps, using the collocations above.

1 Most teachers think it is important to give students _instant feedback_ when they have done a presentation.
2 I was unable to sleep last night due to the .... coming out of the club down the road.
3 The dancers were young and enthusiastic and the .... of their performance thrilled the audience.
4 I've never seen my sister wearing ....; the way she dresses is often bizarre.
5 The minister had to deal with .... when he introduced the new pension rules.
6 As soon as Peter painted his first picture, his .... as an artist became obvious.
7 We had an unexpectedly .... across the States last year as there were flash floods.
8 We all loved the book; it was such a .... that none of us could put it down.
9 Lucy always spoke her mind and I always found her .... rather refreshing.
10 Jane has very .... of administrative work and should have no difficulty obtaining work in London.

Picture yourself

Synonyms for common adjectives

2 Match the adjectives in the box with the adjectives below which have a similar meaning.

> absorbing   appalling   awesome   chaotic
> complex   convincing   disastrous   ~~gorgeous~~
> gripping   hilarious   humorous   muddled
> plausible   sophisticated   splendid
> staggering   stunning   unpredictable

1 beautiful   gorgeous   ....
2 believable   ....
3 complicated   ....
4 confused   ....
5 funny   ....
6 interesting   ....
7 surprising   ....
8 terrible   ....
9 wonderful   ....

Writing | Part 2
A review

1a Here are some expressions an exam candidate used in a film review. Mark each one according to whether you think they are most likely to be positive (✓) or negative (✗).

A are simply stunning ....✓........
B really bothered me ....
C this lack of ....
D simply do not move me ....
E manages very ably to ....
F is nothing but ....
G was really impressed ....
H pleasantly surprised me ....
I literally lose the plot ....
J with a depressing sense of ....

b Read the film review written by an exam candidate and then complete the gaps, using the expressions A–J from exercise 1a.

I have been asked to write a review of the best and worst films I have seen, and for me personally selecting the two movies is not at all hard. Without doubt, the best film I have ever watched is *Alien*. Special effects without a gripping story (1) ......simply do not move me...... and I usually avoid Hollywood blockbusters, but *Alien* (2) .... It combines two of my favourite film genres, given that it is an awesome science fiction film that is also an absorbing thriller. Subsequently the director (3) .... create a convincing atmosphere of fear, while teaching us a valuable lesson about the beast we all hide inside. The actors' performances are splendid, especially that of Sigourney Weaver, who is the leading actress. The costumes are well designed and the special effects (4) ....

In complete contrast, the worst film I have ever watched is *200 Warriors*. This film (5) .... a disastrous combination of special effects with a chaotic story. Initially I (6) .... by the colourful explosions and the epic battles between the good and evil immortal warriors, but in the end too many events take place and too few plausible explanations are given. As a result, you (7) .... For me, (8) .... a strong storyline is a major fault. Another issue that (9) .... is that there is not a single complex character to identify with and no sophisticated ideas to think about and you therefore emerge from the cinema (10) .... dissatisfaction.

Reading and Use of English | Part 1

For questions **1–8**, read the text below and decide which answer (**A**, **B**, **C** or **D**) best fits each gap. There is an example at the beginning (**0**).

Example:

0 A angle   B appearance   C aspect   D air

THE KOGOD COURTYARD

At the Smithsonian Institute in Washington, the most striking **(0)** .... of the new Kogod courtyard is its canopy roof. This vast undulating glass canopy is **(1)** .... by eight aluminium columns, and carefully designed to **(2)** .... in with the original stonework. The wave-like structure, the first of its **(3)** .... in the world, is constructed of deep, diamond-shaped glass panes, packed around the sides with recycled cotton to act as sound insulation. This **(4)** .... near perfect conditions for musical performances in the courtyard.

From inside the courtyard, clouds and aircraft are clearly **(5)** .... through the canopy. But closer inspection reveals a milky surface covered in enamel dots, which **(6)** .... about two thirds of the light, **(7)** .... helping to keep the courtyard cool during the baking hot Washington summers.

Water is also a vital element of the design. When no event is being held, a wafer-thin 'river' flows through the courtyard, **(8)** .... the visiting children who splash in it. The whole space is designed to be free, accessible and multi-purpose.

1 A carried   B supported   C sustained   D propped
2 A blend   B merge   C combine   D mix
3 A class   B kind   C brand   D set
4 A causes   B leaves   C makes   D creates
5 A visible   B evident   C apparent   D obvious
6 A puts down   B cuts out   C cuts down   D puts out
7 A until   B however   C even   D thus
8 A diverting   B enjoying   C delighting   D rejoicing

Reading and Use of English | Part 3

For questions **1–8**, read the text below. Use the word given in capitals at the end of some of the lines to form a word that fits in the gap in the same line. There is an example at the beginning (**0**).

Performance Art

Performance Art began in the 1960s in the United States as a term used to describe a live event that often included poets, (0) ......*musicians*...... and film-makers, in addition to visual artists. **MUSIC**

There were earlier (1) .... for this art form, including the Bauhaus **PRECEDE**
in Germany, whose members used live theatre workshops to explore the
(2) .... between space, sound and light. By 1970, Performance Art **RELATION**
was a (3) .... term and its definition had become more specific. **GLOBE**
Performances had to be live and they had to be art, not theatre.

Performance artists saw their movement as a means of taking art directly to
the public, thus eliminating the need for galleries, agents and (4) .... **ACCOUNT**
In effect, it became a social commentary on the need to maintain the absolute
(5) .... of art. **PURE**

One (6) .... recent form of Performance Art is 'mobbing', an **COMPARE**
email-driven experiment in organising groups of people who suddenly
(7) .... in public places, interact briefly with others, and then **MATERIAL**
disappear just as (8) .... as they appeared. **EXPECT**

Listening | Part 1

08 You will hear three different extracts. For questions **1–6**, choose the answer (**A**, **B** or **C**) which fits best according to what you hear. There are two questions for each extract.

Extract One
You hear two friends talking about a book.

1 What do the friends agree about?
   A They find the characters in the book very convincing.
   B They immediately found the storyline absorbing.
   C They would like to see the place where the book was set.

2 According to the woman what is the author's reason for writing the book?
   A to explore a new aspect of human psychology
   B to show that people have different interpretations of the same event
   C to make an interesting point that no one has made before

Extract Two
You hear two people talking about a piece of jewellery.

3 What does the man say about the origins of his bracelet?
   A It was chosen as a way to thank him for his hard work.
   B It shows that his uncle had a good opinion of him.
   C It shows he is a man of high rank.

4 The woman understands that, for the man, the bracelet represents
   A the importance of having clear goals.
   B the role he will have in the future.
   C the need to help other people.

Extract Three
You hear two women talking about clothes for a special occasion.

5 They both agree that
   A the dress Louise tries on is a rather unflattering colour.
   B trouser suits always look like office wear.
   C pashminas are a very adaptable clothing accessory.

6 What do we learn about Jack's attitude to clothes?
   A He is not worried about his appearance.
   B He rarely buys expensive clothes.
   C He disapproves of designer clothing.

7 Leisure and entertainment

Grammar
Ways of linking ideas

1 Read this article from a magazine and then complete the gaps, using one of the words or phrases from the box below.

> accepting   arriving   given that   fascinating   how
> if   in ways that   in which   laid out   provided   ~~that is~~
> therefore   what/what   when   whose   unless   yet

MAKING THE MOST OF MUSEUMS

Nowadays there is an increasing emphasis on the idea of life-long education, (1) ..that is.. to say, education that continues through the whole of adulthood. One way (2) .... adults can develop their interest in a new subject is to search the Internet. A potentially much richer way is to wander through a learning environment, such as a science museum, (3) .... in a systematic way to introduce visitors to particular subjects. With the help of audio-visual aids, computer-assisted instruction and other devices, a museum can bring a subject alive (4) .... compare favourably with a television programme, or a book. The kind of help that museums can give to adults can equally well be given to children, and to teachers (5) .... pupils have come to the museum for specific purposes.

At a time (6) .... the demand for public accountability has never been greater, it is worth remembering that many museums receive substantial grants towards (7) .... is supposed to be stimulating educational provision for the general public.

Museums (8) .... these grants, (9) .... offering little more than the occasional public lecture, or very minimal help to schoolteachers (10) .... at the museum with their pupils, (11) .... risk having such financial support severely cut back, or even withdrawn.

Why is this done? The idea is that museums should not simply be aiming to be popular and entertaining, they should also be truly rewarding learning environments. (12) .... this is their aim, they should not just dispense facts and theories. They should show the visitor exactly (13) .... to do with the information (14) .... Isolated snippets of information, (15) .... as they may be, do not encourage museum visitors to use their intelligence. For example, (16) .... told that some fleas can jump 130 times their own height, visitors simply have no idea of (17) .... to apply this knowledge (18) .... they are clearly pointed in the right direction.

2 Complete the sentences with the most suitable form of the participle (present, past or present perfect), using the verbs in brackets. In some sentences, there may be two possible correct answers.

1 ......Looking...... (*look*) round the concert hall, I was surprised to see several people I knew in the audience.
2 .... (*decide*) not to go and play tennis, the two friends went out for a meal.
3 .... (*build*) 2,000 years ago, the Roman amphitheatre is still magnificent.
4 .... (*know*) by everyone as an outstanding speaker, it was no surprise when my uncle was chosen to deliver a public lecture.
5 'Underfunding is the reason for the youth employment scheme .... (*reach*) crisis point over the last few weeks,' said the treasurer at the annual meeting.
6 .... (*view*) through a telescope, the tall ship looked absolutely magnificent.
7 .... (*not care*) about who might overhear her, Caroline said exactly what she thought.
8 .... (*stare*) hard at the horizon, I could just make out the tallest of the mountains.
9 .... (*write*) 50 years ago, the novel addresses issues still of relevance today.
10 .... (*find*) that he had run out of money, Peter realised there was no point in staying in town any longer.
11 .... (*develop*) a new type of drug, the researchers found it caused few side effects in patients.
12 .... (*not understand*) what the instructor was saying, one student put his hand up to ask a question.

Vocabulary
Money expressions

1a Match the two halves of the sentence.

1 Installing double glazing pays for itself
2 It's difficult to make ends meet,
3 If you regularly eat too much,
4 If you want designer clothes
5 I want to pay my way
6 All that extra training for the race
7 Paying £5 for a coffee in the main square
8 The company only just managed

a is really paying dividends.
b is definitely a rip-off.
c so let's split the bill.
d you'll pay through the nose for them.
e because regular heating bills are reduced.
f to break even this year.
g when you're earning a low wage.
h you'll pay the price by putting on weight.

b Which expression means

1 saves the money it cost? ......pay for itself......
2 to be highly over-priced? ....
3 spend too much on something? ....
4 not making a profit or a loss? ....
5 contribute your share of the cost? ....
6 to live on what you earn? ....
7 is getting good results? ....
8 experience a bad result from doing something? ....

Leisure and entertainment

Writing | Part 2
An email

1a Read this email written by an exam candidate.

1. Who is Sam? What was his email about and who did he send it to?
   Who is Chris? Why is the email informal in style?

b For questions 1–12, choose the most suitable word or phrase.

To: samb@rklf.com
From: Chris
▶ **Subject:** Helping at KidZone

Dear Sam,

This is in **(1)** *answer / reply / request* to the email you sent round to everyone asking whether any new students were interested in getting **(2)** *involved / engaged / committed* in the activities being organised to **(3)** *earn / raise / gain* funds for KidZone, the local children's charity. I really enjoy doing charity work and I'd certainly be more than happy to **(4)** *help / carry / give* out with that. I've also got some suggestions to **(5)** *check over / look into / put forward* which you may find helpful.

First, I've got previous experience of a charity cycle race during my last year at school, and I thought we could possibly organise something similar here at the university. We managed to get **(6)** *assets / sponsorship / expenses* from local companies in **(7)** *exchange / trade / deal* for free publicity and product placement. We found that everyone was very pleased to support us once they knew what we were doing was in **(8)** *benefit / aid / assistance* of a good cause!

Another thought I had was that we could approach some individuals who are fairly **(9)** *profitable / well-off / moneyed* and ask if they could each **(10)** *attribute / donate / devote* £100. We could offer them a visit and lunch at KidZone in return. Alternatively, we could **(11)** *dream / draw / get* up a list of play equipment that would be of **(12)** *use / usage / usefulness* to the KidZone centre and ask individuals to buy one piece of equipment of their choice.

If you like my ideas, or would like me to help with anything else, give me a call on 0884723795.

Look forward to hearing from you!

Chris Foxton

Reading and Use of English | Part 8

You are going to read four album reviews from a world music website. For questions **1–10**, choose from the reviews (**A–D**). The reviews may be chosen more than once.

In which review is the following mentioned?

the rapid transition from one source of inspiration to another	1
the high standards a performer is capable of in a certain style	2
the varying focus and linguistic origins of the songs	3
an opening track which impresses without vocals	4
the high standards of musicianship maintained throughout the album	5
the possible problems that can arise from relying on a multitude of sources	6
a decline in standards after some effective tracks	7
the calm atmosphere created by two tracks on the same album	8
the special contribution of a singer to a blend of sounds	9
tracks sequenced in a way that would reflect the performers' wishes	10

World MUSIC REVIEWS: ARTISTS and ALBUMS

A Watcha Clan:
Diaspora Hi-Fi – A Mediterranean Caravan

The album begins with a scrambled montage of voices and Arabic strings and percussion; right away, the listener is projected into a mix of dance floor sounds. This is fusion music, dubbed and electroed. *Watcha Clan* put forward a dilemma: can diverse influences result in a harmonious whole? Or does it just end up as a mish-mash of indistinguishable sound? They certainly add a rich variety of flavours to the dominant rhythms.

Some people can't get enough of vocalist Sista K's unusual voice, but for others even a little is too much. Nassim Kouti sometimes accompanies her on vocals and guitar. One of these tracks is the melodic haunting 'Ch'ilet La'Yani'. The beginning of 'Oued El Chouli' is equally tranquil and briefly entrances before the reggae beat takes over, powered by Moroccan castanets. The song stands out on the album because the really impressive combination of styles works so well.

B Various artists:
Nigeria Disco Funk Special

At one time, would-be artists flocked to Nigeria from all over Africa to put their very individual spin on imported music. The first number on this compilation, an instrumental by *Sahara All Stars* entitled 'Take Your Soul', is bravely funky and strikes just the right opening note. The next outstanding track is by the talented Johnny Haastrup, who gives a great rendition of 'Greetings'. It is hard to understand why he never really made it as a soloist: his treatment of the song is lyrical, and this piece is both harmonic and flamboyant.

Sadly, the remaining songs are variable, and not in the same league, and you may be disappointed that they lack a truly authentic and traditional feel. Also, the material is mostly instrumental, so there are few singing stars in evidence. But despite this, the album is well worth listening to. It's arranged in an order suitable for clubs, which is doubtless what the artists originally intended.

C Neco Novellas:
Khu Kata

Neco Novellas is a singer-songwriter with immense talent and imposing stage presence. His new album, 'Khu Kata', presents influences of his teenage years in Mozambique. Guest vocalist Lilian Vieira of Zuco 103 enriches the track called 'Vermelha' which is a successful mix of Brazilian samba and Mozambican pop. But with 'Phumela' things slide downhill for a while, and the lyrics of 'Swile Navo' can only be described as banal and repetitive.

He returns to form with 'The Train', which is beautifully arranged and owes an obvious debt to the Hugh Masekela songbook ('Stimela!'), but the best tracks are the uplifting 'Tikona' and 'O Sol', which truly stand out as the blend of world/jazz fusion that this artist regularly delivers. Nonetheless, 'Khu Kata' would have been improved by more rigorous editing and slightly fewer tracks.

D Think of One:
Camping Shaabi

Think Of One is truly unique. Over the years, this Antwerp-based group have worked and recorded with a wide range of artists such as Afro-Brazilian percussionists and Inuit throat singers, but for this album, they return to Moroccan themes. The Moroccan effect is apparent straight away in the spellbinding rhythmic voices of the first track, 'J'étais Jetée'. And that's just for starters – the recording goes on to mix diverse sounds and types of music at an astounding speed.

The quality doesn't falter from one track to the next and each track is innovative in its own way. The vintage keyboards and Balkan-style brass section are always there, laying the foundations for the other sounds which are brought in and used around them. In a dazzling combination of Flemish, French, Arabic and English, the band's lyrics also fascinate, some having a serious tone and others being more frivolous, but a singable tune always surfaces.

Listening | Part 2

09 You will hear a professional dancer giving a talk to performing arts students about dancing as a career. For questions **1–8**, complete the sentences with a word or short phrase.

DANCING

To become a (1) .... dancer, it is best to start lessons when you are very young.

On degree courses, there is often more emphasis on academic learning than (2) .... skills.

In order to make contacts, dance students should attend (3) ....

For auditions, dancers should prepare questions as well as focus on (4) .... and appearance.

Dancers must be prepared to experience (5) .... during their careers and develop other skills.

Some dancers are reluctant to consider (6) .... as a way of earning money.

Dancers should try to avoid (7) .... which may shorten a career.

Dancers who are unwilling to (8) .... are unlikely to do well.

8 Media matters

Grammar
Reported speech

1a Read the article below and then write what the people actually said to the reporter in the speech balloons which follow.

The rise of commuter television

Rail commuters fed up with shouts of 'I'm on a train', the hum of music players and mobile ringtones now have another challenge – televisions. Many commuters are already used to TVs in the carriages but televisions are going to be installed in our local commuter trains for the first time. We got on the 8.18 to Manchester to find out what people thought about this.

James French, 25, said he'd been commuting for the last year and he thought it was a pretty good idea because he could watch it if he wanted. If he didn't want to, he'd read a book but his worst nightmare would be constant sport.

Sophie Morton, 17, who travels to school every day, agreed they were a good thing. She said she would stop listening to music and watch the news instead, which meant she would be learning something on her way to school.

But most commuters were not keen on the idea.

Natasha Gordon, 27, is American and she said she'd travelled on lots of trains in the US with TV in them and she'd hated it. She wanted to know why the money was being spent on TV when it could go towards improvements in basic services.

Francesco Vecchi, 42, explained that he had to catch the train to work and he objected to TV being forced on him. He was concerned that he wouldn't be able to do vital reading for his job.

We put these points to **Jason O'Donovan**, spokesperson for the railway company. He said that they would never put TV in every carriage and they were going to trial it first as it might be popular in some trains but not others.

> I've been commuting for the last year and I think it's a pretty good idea because I can watch it if I want. If I don't want to, I'll read a book but my worst nightmare would be constant sport.

James French

Sophie Morton

Natasha Gordon

Francesco Vecchi

Jason O'Donovan

Media matters

b The reporter summarised his article for the front page of his newspaper. Here are the questions he asked. Use the questions to complete what he wrote.

1. Are you happy about having TV in the train?
2. What do you usually do during your journey?
3. Would you enjoy watching TV on the train?
4. Do you travel on this train every day?
5. How long have you been commuting?

Commuters' responses to TV idea

I wanted to find out (1) *if commuters were happy about having TV in the train.* I asked them (2) .... journey. Most of them seemed to read or listen to music. I wanted to know (3) .... watching TV on the train. Most of them didn't think so. I asked them (4) .... every day and (5) .... Most people used the train every day and some had been commuting for years.

2 Read what these people said and then complete the reported sentences, using a verb from the box below in the past tense.

| advise | ~~announce~~ | complain | deny | doubt | enquire |
| urge | warn |

1. 'There will be an extra public holiday next month.' The *President announced (that) there would be an extra public holiday the following month* .
2. 'Are there any job vacancies in the company?' The man ....
3. 'We're being given far too much work.' The students ....
4. 'Don't eat a large meal before going for a run.' The fitness instructor .... his trainees ....
5. 'I didn't tell Frankie the news.' Joe ....
6. 'If I were you, I'd ring Laurie before you turn up.' Rachel .... them ....
7. 'Recycle as much paper as you can.' The company .... its employees ....
8. 'I don't think Ruth is telling the truth.' Jamie ....

Vocabulary
Television, newspapers and computers

Read the definitions from the *Cambridge Advanced Learner Dictionary* which follow and then use the letters below to make the correct word.

CODTAPS	GIPTOTLHS	GOGBELR	LOBADIT
LULBINET	MORECLICAM	NOTATENTCS	PESIODE
SBADTOCAR	~~IRPISC~~

1. *script* : the words of a film, play or speech

2. .... : to send out a programme on television or radio

3. .... : a short news programme often about something that has just happened

4. .... : a pre-recorded audio programme that's posted to a website and made available for download

5. .... : a type of popular newspaper with small pages which has many pictures

6. .... : an advertisement on television or radio

7. .... : someone who produces an ongoing narrative, similar to a diary

8. .... : people who receive a lot of public attention are said to be in this

9. .... : someone who competes, often in a quiz

10. .... : one of the single parts into which a story is divided on TV or radio

Writing | Part 2
A proposal

Read the proposal written by an exam candidate and then choose the correct word or expression for 1-12.

I am absolutely (1) *assured / convinced / persuaded* that (2) *committed / constant / regular* listeners to RadioTen will be delighted to tune in to the series of eight programmes you are making about our region. You (3) *requested / asked / required* some suggestions about content for the programmes, and here are mine:

1 The history of the local population

People often (4) *discuss / express / comment* that the history of our region is extremely rich, but they only ever (5) *talk / mention / tell* the last two or three hundred years. In fact, our region has a history dating back to prehistoric times, and I believe it would be very interesting to make a programme examining each of the key historical periods from the (6) *outlook / perspective / opinion* of an ordinary person who lived at that time. An actor could give a detailed personal (7) *discussion / account / commentary* of daily life for that individual, which the presenter could then go on to (8) *express / discuss / mention*.

2 The continuing development of farming

This programme could be linked to the historical theme I (9) *referred / outlined / planned* above, with the presenter (10) *admitting / emphasising / asserting* what farming was like at different periods in our regional history. The final part of the programme could briefly (11) *question / address / talk* the issue of global warming, and how it will impact on the type of crops our region produces.

I trust my recommendations will meet with your approval; they would, I believe, (12) *attract / appeal / adhere* to both local listeners and a much broader audience. They could therefore create more interest in our region. As there is certainly potential for increased tourism and business investment, this would be very helpful.

Reading and Use of English | Part 2

For questions **1–8**, read the text below and think of the word which best fits each gap. Use only **one** word in each gap. There is an example at the beginning (**0**).

Effects of television on childhood literacy

Nowadays, television occupies a large portion (0) ......*of*...... children's time. From when they start in preschool, children spend more time watching television than participating in any other activity (1) .... sleeping. However, this is not necessarily a bad thing.

The results of some research suggest that there is considerable overlap (2) .... the comprehension processes activated while reading and the processes that take place (3) .... a period of television viewing. If this is (4) ...., it may very well (5) .... the case that children who learn comprehension skills from television viewing before they are ready to read are equipped (6) .... some very important tools when they later learn to read.

It has been noted that children are frequently better at recalling televised stories they have watched compared to those they have simply heard. (7) .... to the fact that it is a visual medium, television can present information more concretely than written and spoken text, making it an ideal medium in (8) .... to cultivate some of the skills and knowledge needed for later reading.

Media matters

Reading and Use of English | Part 4

For questions **1–6**, complete the second sentence so that it has a similar meaning to the first sentence, using the word given. **Do not change the word given**. You must use between **three** and **six** words, including the word given. Here is an example (**0**).

Example:

0 There needs to be tighter control than there is at present over what happens in reality TV programmes.
   TIGHTLY
   Reality TV programmes should be ……… *more tightly controlled* ……… than they are at present.

1 News programmes should not be allowed to show disturbing images in the early evening.
   PREVENTED
   News programmes should ……………………………… disturbing images in the early evening.

2 I eventually managed to persuade Louisa that I was telling the truth.
   SUCCEEDED
   I eventually ……………………………… Louisa that I was telling the truth.

3 George felt a sense of pride in the achievements of the family business.
   PROUD
   George ……………………………… the family business had achieved.

4 Unless the director gets the actor he wants for the main part, the film will be cancelled.
   MEAN
   If the director doesn't get the actor he wants for the main part, it ……………………………… the film.

5 The reliability of the Internet as a source of information is sometimes difficult to determine.
   HOW
   It is sometimes difficult to determine ……………………………… as a source of information.

6 The employees suggested some improvements to the computer system which would make it easier to use.
   FORWARD
   The employees ……………………………… improving the computer system to make it easier to use.

Listening | Part 4

▶ 10 You will hear five short extracts in which people are talking about their jobs in television.

TASK ONE

For questions **1–5**, choose from the list (**A–H**) each speaker's job.

TASK TWO

For questions **6–10**, choose from the list (**A–H**) what each speaker says they find difficult about their job.

While you listen you must complete both tasks.

A make-up artist
B producer
C actor
D researcher
E sports presenter
F lighting engineer
G sound technician
H costume designer

Speaker 1 [1]
Speaker 2 [2]
Speaker 3 [3]
Speaker 4 [4]
Speaker 5 [5]

A having to upset people
B incorporating last-minute changes
C not getting enough variety
D listening to people's problems
E being told what to do
F keeping up to date
G not getting enough recognition
H working in uncomfortable conditions

Speaker 1 [6]
Speaker 2 [7]
Speaker 3 [8]
Speaker 4 [9]
Speaker 5 [10]

9 At top speed

Grammar
Tenses in time clauses and time adverbials

1a Read the article below and then choose the correct word or phrase.

THE HISTORY of GRAND PRIX RACING

Grand Prix racing has its roots in organised automobile racing that began in France **(1)** *as far back as* / *as long as* 1894. Organisers were keen to exploit motor racing as a showcase for their cars, and the first race, which took place **(2)** *in* / *on* July 22 of that year, organised by a Paris newspaper, **(3)** *was held* / *had been held* over the 128-km distance between Paris and Rouen. On that occasion, although Jules de Dion won the race, he **(4)** *was not given* / *had not been given* the prize because his car **(5)** *has relied* / *relied* on a mechanical stoker, a device for putting coal into a boiler.
(6) *During* / *Meanwhile* James Gordon Bennett Jnr established the Gordon Bennett Cup in the USA, hoping that the creation of such an international event would encourage manufacturers to improve their cars. However, it was **(7)** *only when* / *not until* 1906 that the Automobile Club de France organised a Grand Prix on a circuit in Le Mans. The race **(8)** *was won* / *had been won* by the Hungarian-born Ferenc Szisz in a Renault.

In this **(9)** *period* / *time*, races were heavily nationalistic affairs, with a few countries setting up races of their own, but no formal championship holding them together. The cars all had a mechanic on board as well as a driver, and these two **(10)** *allowed* / *were allowed* to work on the cars **(11)** *during* / *over* the race. Races **(12)** *were run* / *were being run* over a lengthy circuit of closed public roads, rather than purpose-built tracks, and given the state of the roads **(13)** *at* / *by* this time, repairs were a common occurrence. Grand Prix races gradually spread through Europe and the US, and in 1924, the many national motor clubs banded together to form an association (AIACR) which was empowered to regulate Grand Prix and other forms of international racing.
Eventually Grand Prix racing **(14)** *evolved* / *was evolving* into formula racing, and the Formula One so popular now can be seen as its direct descendant. **(15)** *In* / *To* this day, each event in the Formula One World Championships is still called a Grand Prix.

b Match the two halves of the sentence.

1 I'll be drafting our presentation
2 As soon as I've finished my essay,
3 He read most of the novel
4 When I know the answer to your question,
5 I'll talk to the electrician about the problem
6 He'll be coming straight home
7 By the time I'd collected all the statistics,
8 As soon as they'd come to an agreement,
9 The top player injured his wrist
10 I'll get some new strings for my guitar

a while we were all travelling back on the train.
b while you draw up the graphs we need for it.
c I took the contract down to the legal office.
d I'll hand it in to my tutor.
e there wasn't time to finish the report.
f while he was serving for the set.
g while we're out shopping together in town.
h when he's finished his shift at the hospital.
i I'll tell you what it is.
j as soon as I see him tomorrow.

Time expressions with *at*, *in* and *on*

2 👁 Complete the sentences with the correct preposition.

1. Maria met her future husband ....**in**......... the early nineties.
2. Not everyone is willing to work overtime .... weekends.
3. The technican is here .... Mondays and Fridays.
4. A positive attitude will bring great results .... the end.
5. I performed badly because I wasn't sleeping well .... night.
6. It's always difficult to know what to do .... your first evening in a new city.
7. Most of my friends look forward to watching football .... Saturday afternoons.
8. .... the beginning of the week I was not absolutely sure I would enjoy my new job.
9. My company is overloaded with printing work .... certain times of day.
10. A good knowledge of several languages will help us .... the future.

Writing | Part 1
An essay

1 Read the exam task below.

> Your class has attended a panel discussion on what methods local authorities should use to limit the use of cars.
>
> **What methods could local authorities use to limit the use of cars?**
> - public transport
> - education
> - charges
>
> Some opinions expressed in the discussion:
>
> 'Cars are convenient.'
>
> 'People don't realise the impact individuals make.'
>
> 'Making people pay to drive through cities is a good idea.'
>
> Write an essay for your tutor discussing **two** of the methods in your notes. You should explain **which method you think is more important** for local authorities to consider and give reasons to support your opinion. You may, if you wish, use the opinions expressed in the discussion, but you should use your own words as far as possible.

2a Complete the gaps in the essay, choosing expressions from the box.

b Tick the two methods mentioned in the essay and the opinion that was discussed.

c Which method did the candidate think was the most successful and why?

> accordingly   an additional benefit   another way of
> in combination   in conclusion   moreover   nevertheless
> resulting in   therefore   ~~there is no doubt that~~
> this means that   to some extent

Nowadays an increasing number of people own and drive cars and in many cities this has become a real problem causing traffic jams and slow journeys.

One obvious solution is for local authorities to spend more on public transport. (1) *There is no doubt that* this is the most effective method of moving people from one part of a city to another. A lot of money has been invested in buses and trams in many places and (2) .... this has been successful. (3) .... , even when there is an excellent public transport system available, many people still seem to prefer their own cars and fewer people use public transport than might be expected. This, (4) .... , might not be the best way to persuade people to leave their cars at home.

(5) .... approaching the problem is to introduce a fee system. (6) .... drivers have to pay every time they go into the city and it makes them think before they get into their car. (7) .... , they tend to make fewer journeys by car. (8) .... , they may even try to share journeys to work with other people, (9) .... a reduction in the number of cars during peak times. (10) .... to bringing in a charge is that people may walk for some or part of their journey.

(11) .... , I think a system which charges people to drive into a city is a good first step to limiting the number of cars. (12) .... with this, money also needs to be invested in buses, cycle lanes and pedestrian streets to enable people to get around.

Vocabulary

Expressions with *in*

Complete the sentences below with an appropriate noun from the box.

accordance   aid   ~~event~~   form   hope   light   position   region

1 In the ……event…… of an emergency, all passengers are requested to assemble on the lower deck.
2 In the ……………………… of recent information, the government has revised its plans for educational reform.
3 The buyers were finally in a ……………………… to go ahead with the purchase of the property.
4 We have amended the contract in ……………………… with your recent instructions.
5 Maria mentioned her desire for further training in the ……………………… that her company would fund it.
6 A concert was arranged in ……………………… of the local children's home.
7 Compensation was offered in the ……………………… of a credit voucher.
8 A flat in the centre of the city will cost in the ……………………… of £1,000 a month to rent.

Reading and Use of English | Part 5

You are going to read an article about the life of John Paul Stapp. For questions **1–6**, choose the answer (**A**, **B**, **C** or **D**) which you think fits best according to the text.

JOHN PAUL STAPP:
THE SCIENCE of AVIATION

Captain John Paul Stapp, already a medical doctor, began his scientific career in the 1940s studying the negative effects of high-altitude flight, issues absolutely critical to the future of aviation. How could men survive these conditions? The problem of the bends, the deadly formation of bubbles in the bloodstream, proved the toughest, but after 65 hours in the air, Stapp found an answer. If a pilot breathed pure oxygen for 30 minutes prior to take-off, symptoms could be avoided entirely.

line 9   This was an enormous breakthrough. The sky now truly was the limit. The discovery pushed Stapp to the forefront of the Aero Med Lab and he abandoned his plans to become a pediatrician, instead deciding to dedicate his life to research. The Lab's mandate, to study medical and safety issues in aviation, was a perfect match for his talents. It was the premiere facility in the world for the new science of biomechanics.

Stapp was assigned the Lab's most important research project: human deceleration. This was the study of the human body's ability to withstand G forces, the force of gravity, when bailing out of an aircraft. In April 1947, Stapp travelled to Los Angeles to view the 'human decelerator', a rocket sled designed to run along a special track and then come to a halt with the aid of 45 sets of normal hydraulic brakes, which slowed it from 150 miles per hour to half of that speed in one fifth of a second. When it did, G forces would be produced equivalent to those experienced in an airplane crash. The sled was called

1 What does the writer mean when he says 'The sky now truly was the limit' (lines 9–10)?
   A Stapp had set an unbeatable scientific record.
   B All previous restrictions on flight had been removed.
   C Pilots could now be trained to fly at greater altitude.
   D A new design was needed for high-altitude planes.

2 What assessment of Stapp's skills does the writer make in the first paragraph?
   A He was a better scientist than his contemporaries.
   B He was able to solve scientific problems at great speed.
   C He was able to prove a theory set out by others.
   D He was ideally suited to employment at Aero Med Lab.

3 What was surprising about the construction of Gee Whiz?
   A It incorporated a revolutionary new kind of brakes.
   B It was initially designed to function without a passenger.
   C It could tolerate exceptionally high G forces.
   D It was not built of conventional materials.

4 Why did Stapp usually insist on doing test runs on Gee Whiz himself?
   A He felt his powers of observation were superior to those of other people.
   B He was aware that some people were psychologically unsuited to the tests.
   C He had little faith in the overall safety of the equipment.
   D He thought it was unethical to recruit people for a dangerous task.

5 What was the significance of the experiments on Sonic Wind No. 1?
   A They broke all previous speed records.
   B They gradually improved deceleration times.
   C They set new limits to human potential.
   D They proved that most people would survive high speeds.

6 In this text, the writer implies that Stapp's main motivation was
   A a desire to minimise loss of life.
   B a spirit of adventure.
   C a quest for expertise.
   D a wish to be remembered after his death.

---

the 'Gee Whiz'. Built out of welded tubes, it was designed to withstand 100 Gs of force, way beyond the 18 Gs that accepted theory of the time thought survivable. Early tests were conducted using a dummy, but Stapp soon insisted that conditions were right to use himself as a human guinea pig.

Exercising a modicum of caution on the first ride in December 1947, Stapp used only one rocket. The Gee Whiz barely reached 90 miles an hour, and the deceleration was only about 10 Gs. So Stapp began to increase the number of rockets, and by August 1948, he had completed 16 runs, surviving not just 18 Gs but a bone-jarring 35 Gs. Battered though he was by the tests, Stapp was reluctant to allow anyone else to ride the Gee Whiz. He feared that if certain people, especially test pilots, were used, their hot-headedness might produce a disaster. Volunteers made some runs, but whenever a new approach was developed, Stapp was his own one and only choice as test subject. There was one obvious benefit: Stapp could write extremely accurate physiological and psychological reports concerning the effects of his experiments.

Yet while the Gee Whiz allowed Stapp to answer the existing deceleration questions, new ones emerged. What could be done to help pilots ejecting from supersonic aircraft to survive? Stapp set out to find the answer on a new sled called Sonic Wind No. 1, which could travel at 750 miles per hour, and withstand an astonishing 150 Gs. In January 1954, Stapp embarked on a series of runs leading to his 29th and final ride, which took him to above the speed of sound, protected only by a helmet and visor. And when the sled stopped, in a mere 1.4 seconds, Stapp was subjected to more Gs than anyone had ever willingly endured. He wasn't just proving that people could survive a high-speed ejection, he was establishing the parameters of human survivability to G force: new biological boundaries were being set.

That successful run on 10 December 1954 provided Colonel Stapp with an opportunity he had longed for – to promote the cause of automobile safety. Stapp had long realised that his research was just as applicable to cars as it was to airplanes. At every opportunity, Stapp urged the car industry to examine his crash data, and to design their cars with safety in mind. He lobbied hard for the installation of seat belts and improvements such as collapsing steering wheels. 'I'm leading a crusade for the prevention of needless deaths,' he told *Time* magazine in 1955.

Stapp's work in aeronautics and automobiles continued right up until his death in 1999 at age 89. He had received numerous awards and honors. But the best was the knowledge that his work had helped to save many lives, not just in aviation, but on highways around the world.

Listening | Part 2

▶11 You will hear a zoology student called Anna Samuels giving a presentation to other students about a trip she made to find out about cheetahs, the fastest-moving large cats in Africa. For questions **1–8**, complete the sentences with a word or short phrase.

CHEETAHS

Volunteers were required to be **(1)** .... , due to the number of different jobs that need doing.

Anna particularly appreciated being able to **(2)** .... out of doors.

Anna mentions a **(3)** .... to explain the way a cheetah's feet function.

Anna's work involved using a new kind of **(4)** .... which scientists have developed to track the cheetahs.

Anna collected detailed information about the cheetahs' **(5)** .... , position and speed.

Anna found out that the speed of a cheetah is less important than the way it can **(6)** .... suddenly.

Anna's results showed that **(7)** .... was the most popular time of day for hunting.

Anna was surprised to find out that cheetahs went into areas of **(8)** .... to hunt for food.

10 A lifelong process

Grammar
Expressing ability, possibility and obligation

1 Read this extract from a column in a magazine and then complete the gaps, using *can, must, have to, need* or *be able to* in the correct form – present, perfect or past. Make the verbs negative where you see (*not*) in brackets.

I met someone famous

When my sister Emily was 13, her school arranged an exchange visit with a school in Canada and a girl called Carrie came to stay with us. She lived in a very isolated area in Canada and she was really excited when she saw that a band was going to play in our town hall.

I heard her say to Emily 'This (1) ......*could*...... be my only opportunity this year to see a live band, because at home we (2) .... drive a hundred miles to the nearest big city and so we don't go very often. But you (3) .... (*not*) come if you don't want to.'

Emily was happy to go but she knew our parents wouldn't agree. I'd started at university but luckily it was the holidays and I was at home, so Emily (4) .... (*not*) persuade our parents to let her and Carrie go on their own. Emily and Carrie (5) .... be at school when the tickets went on sale, but I was studying for exams at home so I (6) .... queue outside the hall. I got there before the box office opened, but I (7) .... (*not*) hurried because there was hardly anyone else there and I (8) .... get really good seats. I had no idea if the band would be any good and I warned Carrie 'You (9) .... (*not*) be disappointed because we don't normally get good bands here so they (10) .... be really bad.' She said she didn't mind. The night arrived and the band started playing. As soon as they went on stage, I realised that one of them was the brother of a university friend of mine and when they finished we (11) .... go backstage and meet them. It was a really good night and in fact the band actually became famous. We have souvenir programmes which we (12) .... sell for a lot of money if we wanted to.

2 👁 Look at these sentences written by exam candidates, all of which contain mistakes in the use of modal verbs. Find the mistake in each one and then correct it.

1 The bus got so hot that I felt I ~~can't~~ *couldn't* breathe any more.
2 If you live a long way away, you are able to stay at the college hostel.
3 We don't have to forget how hard women fought to get the vote.
4 I am very sorry but I really couldn't be at the airport when you arrive.
5 When we arrived at the college, we must find our own accommodation.
6 We couldn't wait to see you next week when you come to visit us.
7 I'm determined to work for the company for as long as I'll be able.
8 A lot of my friends have taken their driving test but only a few can pass it on the first attempt.
9 The student study centre isn't as good as it has to be, given the cost of the fees.
10 They wouldn't afford to buy new clothes except on rare occasions.
11 I have received your email and I'm happy to tell you I could help you with your dissertation.
12 You needn't to worry about the tickets as I've already bought them.

Vocabulary
Expressions with prepositions

1a 👁 Look at these sentences written by exam candidates. Each one contains an expression with a preposition. Choose the correct preposition.

1 You'll find all the information you need *at / in /* [*on*] the website.
2 You should wait *at / in / on* the queue until the cashier's light comes on.
3 It's better to sit *at / in / on* the left-hand side of the bus because it's cooler.
4 There's been a huge improvement in the quality of food *at / in / on* the canteen.
5 The bus stop is *at / in / on* the opposite side of the road to my house.
6 I'm a student *at / in / on* a language school in Bristol.
7 At the musical, we sat *at / in / on* the back row and we could hardly see the stage.
8 Please contact me *at / in / on* 76598409932 when my computer is repaired.

49

A lifelong process

b For each sentence, choose the correct noun in these expressions with *at*.

1 When James told me his news I was at a .... about what to say.
  A failure   B loss ☑   C confusion   D trouble
2 You shouldn't accept everything politicians say at face .... as they are often trying to win votes.
  A merit   B value   C worth   D benefit
3 I could tell at a .... that something had upset Sam.
  A glance   B look   C glimpse   D sight
4 If you have to cancel at short .... you will be charged a fee.
  A advice   B warning   C notice   D announcement
5 The children who represented the school at the ceremony were chosen at ....
  A chance   B coincidence   C accident   D random
6 Being a doctor can be very hard at .... because of all the decisions you have to make.
  A periods   B occasions   C times   D moments
7 Not being able to speak any foreign languages puts me at a .... when applying for jobs.
  A disadvantage   B weakness   C drawback   D shortcoming
8 She spent a lot of time playing tennis at the .... of her studies.
  A waste   B cost   C sacrifice   D expense

Word building

2a Make these adjectives into nouns. Use one of these suffixes: *-ance, -ence, -ity,* or *-ness* and make any other necessary changes.

> annoyed   capable   convenient   innocent   lonely
> necessary   pure   ready   reliable   significant   simple

b Change these nouns into adjectives. Use one of these suffixes: *-al, -ic or –ous* and make any other necessary changes.

> chaos   gene   humour   influence   luxury
> nutrition   practice   problem   space   theory

3 Put the words in brackets into the correct form, using one of the suffixes from Exercise 2.

A different kind of education

'Alternative' schools exist in most countries but they are in the
(1) ......minority...... (*minor*). They are often privately funded and
have a particular focus. Many are (2) .... (*residence*), as
children travel some distance to attend them. Some aim to encourage
(3) .... (*creative*), with a large amount of time spent on subjects
which are (4) .... (*artist*) like music or performing arts. Some
have few rules on (5) .... (*attend*) and allow children to decide
for themselves how and when they study. This may result in children
valuing and acknowledging the (6) .... (*relevant*) of education
along with a true (7) .... (*willing*) to learn but it may also
be (8) .... (*disaster*). In mainstream schools there will be an
(9) .... (*aware*) of the range of (10) .... (*able*) and levels of (11) ....
(*competent*) that can be expected from each student in each subject. However, there is a more limited
number of (12) .... (*possible*) available for offering specialised programmes as these schools
usually have to follow a conventional curriculum and may not have insufficient funds.

Writing | Part 2
A report

1a Read this student's report.
1. Who has it been written for?
2. Who has written it?
3. What is the aim of the report?

b Complete the gaps, using the expressions below. Then give each section of the report a heading.

> another important issue   as for   consequently
> in addition   ~~on behalf of~~   one final point
> our top priority   therefore   to begin with   to conclude

I'm writing (1) ......on behalf of...... the student committee to give an assessment of the college library and offer some suggestions for the improvements that we feel are urgently required.

A ....
(2) ...., the library building is extremely dilapidated and in need of complete renovation. The same is true of the furniture: the desks and chairs are extremely worn, and create a very negative impression. (3) .... the environment of the library is not currently very conducive to study.

B ....
(4) .... the range of books, although it is wide, much of the material is now outdated and could be disposed of; this would create more space for extra informal seating or more workstations.

C ....
(5) .... to take into consideration is IT facilities. Most students spend much of their day working independently; an upgrade in IT facilities would (6) .... be of enormous benefit.

D ....
(7) .... is that the opening hours of the library are currently totally inadequate. Students have different learning styles and very varied study patterns; it is thus essential that the library should remain accessible until midnight and open its doors by 7 in the morning.

E ....
(8) ...., we would strongly recommend that the library be refurbished as soon as funding permits. (9) ...., we suggest that the stock of books is rationalised, and the IT system improved. (10) ...., however, would be that the opening hours are extended, which may involve employing additional staff.

Reading and Use of English | Part 2

For questions **1–8**, read the text below and think of the word which best fits each gap. Use only **one** word in each gap. There is an example at the beginning (**0**).

Electronic voting system

Because university lectures are usually attended (0) ......by...... large numbers of students, there is little interaction and (1) .... way for the lecturer to check whether the students are benefiting. However, thanks (2) .... an invention known (3) .... an electronic voting system – or 'clickers' for short – this situation is beginning to change. 'Clickers' are hand-held devices on (4) .... students click the relevant button to answer questions posed by the lecturer. The students' answers are communicated to the lecturer's computer either by infra-red transmitter (5) .... by radio frequency and the results are displayed on the lecturer's projection screen at the front of the hall. Initially lecturers presumed that the advantage of clickers for students would be that they would make lectures an interactive, (6) .... than a passive, experience. But there have been unforeseen advantages for the lecturers themselves because they are much more in touch with (7) .... the students are getting on in the subject. It also seems that students talk to (8) .... other about the content of their lectures much more.

Reading and Use of English | Part 1

For questions **1–8**, read the text below and decide which answer (**A**, **B**, **C** or **D**) best fits each gap. There is an example at the beginning (**0**).

Example:

0 A setting   B fixing   C creating   D directing

Study habits

We have all heard that good study habits involve sitting somewhere quiet, sticking to a schedule and **(0)** .... yourself targets. However, such habits don't work for everyone and cognitive scientists have come up with some new **(1)** .... In fact, the brain makes **(2)** .... associations between what it is studying and the background sensations it has at the time. **(3)** .... study to one place may therefore have **(4)** .... effects because when the context is varied, the information being studied is enriched and forgetting is slowed down. In **(5)** ...., the information is given more support from the multiple associations. Evidence also shows that varying the type of material studied in a single sitting leaves a **(6)** .... impression on the brain than does concentrating on one skill at a time. Musicians have known this for years, as have athletes who routinely **(7)** .... strength, speed and skill drills into their workouts. These ideas seem to work when applied to any subject so it seems time for this **(8)** .... to studying to be taken more seriously.

1 A outcomes	B consequences	C findings	D judgements
2 A thoughtful	B subtle	C sensitive	D influential
3 A Restricting	B Modifying	C Controlling	D Enclosing
4 A hurtful	B detrimental	C destructive	D punishing
5 A honesty	B force	C origin	D effect
6 A fuller	B heavier	C deeper	D bolder
7 A incorporate	B include	C comprise	D unite
8 A procedure	B theory	C concept	D approach

Listening | Part 1

12 You will hear three different extracts. For questions **1–6**, choose the answer (**A**, **B** or **C**) which fits best according to what you hear. There are two questions for each extract.

Extract One

You hear two people talking in a university about studying abroad.

1 What did the woman find most difficult about studying at the French university?
  A the range of subjects
  B the methods of teaching
  C the attitude of the lecturers

2 What decision did the woman make during her time in France?
  A She would make more effort to practise her French.
  B She would spend more time with the friends she'd missed.
  C She would try to make contact with foreign students in England.

Extract Two

You hear two people talking in a shop.

3 What surprised the woman about the products on sale?
  A They cost so much.
  B They seemed very stylish.
  C They were made from recycled materials.

4 What do the speakers agree on about the shop?
  A It has something different to offer.
  B It has copied other similar shops.
  C It will be successful.

Extract Three

You hear an interview with a woman who is a trapeze artist in a circus.

5 What does she find most satisfying about her job?
  A being able to express herself artistically
  B getting a good reaction from the audience
  C experimenting with new movements

6 She compares herself to a pilot because they both need to
  A be adaptable.
  B rely on other people.
  C stay calm.

11 Being somewhere else

Grammar
Conditionals

1a Match the clause on the left to one or more clauses on the right. Find as many correct answers as possible.

1 If you were to find a good guidebook in town, *c, e, g, l*
2 If it hadn't been for the terrible weather,
3 If you would book the flights,
4 If he hadn't been taking so many risks,
5 If she's still refusing to speak about it,
6 If you could arrive early tomorrow,
7 If he's decided against taking the new job,
8 If you'll help me with the supermarket shop,
9 If you've decided not to go to the film,
10 If you don't overheat the coffee,

a we can be home in half an hour.
b you won't ruin the flavour.
c I'd really appreciate it.
d he wouldn't have fallen off his bike.
e we could look for accommodation.
f we might have really enjoyed the holidays.
g could you buy it for me?
h there's no point in asking any more questions.
i he won't be relocating.
j she'd have done some hill-walking.
k he wouldn't be feeling so stupid now.
l do let me know.
m that's fine by me.
n we'll be able to finish it quickly.

b Complete each of these sentences in **two** different ways in your own words, using different tenses or modals.

1 I won't be able to travel much unless
   ....
   ....

2 I'll bring my sports kit to the gym, otherwise
   ....
   ....

3 I'll have to finish this work, or
   ....
   ....

c ▶13 Read this short extract from a conversation about holidays and complete the gaps in the dialogue. Then listen and compare your answers.

A: … but we had an amazing time. So this is one of the pictures I took. The Taj Mahal was absolutely fantastic. Have you ever been there?
B: No, but (1) .... I would! I'd go to India like a shot. I didn't have the money when I was a student, but now I'm working, (2) .... if I have time.
A: Well, I'd certainly recommend going to India. I'm sure (3) .... if you went.
B: And (4) ...., I'll travel around as much as I can, just like you did!
A: Well, I certainly loved every minute of my trip. But I didn't realise how hot it would be in June. If I'd known, (5) ....earlier in the year instead.

Vocabulary
Phrasal verbs: word order with pronouns

1 Finish the second sentence in each pair so it means the same as the first.

1 We wrapped the present up and gave it to Anna immediately.
   We gave the present to Anna as soon as we had wrapped ....*it up*............ .

2 I enrolled for the art class as soon as I saw they were running one.
   As soon as I discovered they were running an art class, I signed ....

3 When the committee heard that Peter couldn't get there, they cancelled the meeting.
   When the committee heard that Peter couldn't get to the meeting, they called ....

4 I couldn't face going to the dentist, so I postponed my appointment.
   I couldn't face going to my dentist appointment, so I put ....

5 As soon as I realised the trip was going to be on Saturday, I decided not to go.
As soon as I realised the trip was going to be on Saturday, I dropped ....

6 Despite not feeling totally ready, I took my driving test as planned.
Although I did not feel totally ready to take my driving test, I went ....

7 I felt elated as I finally left on my long-awaited holiday.
When my long-awaited holiday finally arrived, I felt elated as I set ....

8 No one will allow me to forget that I tripped when I first went on stage.
I tripped as I made my first entrance on stage, and I won't ever live ....

Expressions with *on*

2 Complete the sentences below with an appropriate noun from the box.

air   ball   basis   behalf   board   grounds   hold
horizon   ~~increase~~   loan   location   road   show   site
track

1 Unfortunately, unemployment is on the ......*increase*...... in some countries.
2 There's a subsidised restaurant on .... which all employees can use.
3 On the .... of current evidence, we have no reason to think that the new virus will affect humans.
4 The new drama series is shot on .... in Sweden.
5 Since the programme was being broadcast live on ...., the minister chose his words with care.
6 The building of the new hospital is on .... until more funds are raised.
7 The dean welcomed new students to the biology department on .... of the teaching faculty.
8 We were all relieved to hear that the solution to the traffic problem was finally on the ....
9 The suspect refused to say anything, on the .... that he might incriminate himself.
10 That young entrepreneur is already on .... to become a wealthy man.
11 The recording equipment is on .... and we have to return it immediately after the concert.
12 The students' suggestions were taken on .... by the college and the timetable was reorganised.
13 The architect's plans for the new building are currently on .... in the committee room.
14 By the time we finally came across a petrol station we'd been on the .... for more than five hours.

Writing | Part 2
A review

1a Read the review below. Who is it written for? What is the purpose of the review?

b Choose one of the adjectives below for each of the gaps. Use each adjective only once.

extensive   familiar   gentle   mouth-watering   personal
skilled   soft   ~~spoilt~~   uplifting   vibrant

c There are ten spelling mistakes in the review. Find them and correct them.

There is a wonderful choice of restaurants in our local area, and anyone hoping to enjoy a tasty meal out in plesant *(pleasant)* surroundings is truly (1) ......*spoilt*...... for choice. However, if you are looking for a suitable venue to take company trainees, I would definitly opt for one of the two described below.

The first place I'd recomend is a very informal American-style restaurant called The Food Stop, which has a (2) .... atmosphere and really (3) .... live music. The menu is (4) .... and there is certainley something to suit all tastes, including vegetarian. The waiting staff are very (5) .... at offering appropriate suggestions and explaining new and less (6) .... dishes. It would be a great place for the trainees to unwind and take a brake from the serious atmosphere of the workplace and get to know each other on a more (7) .... level.

The alternatif is a Chinese restaurant called TigerLily which offers a truly (8) .... buffet of cooked dishes. You can also select raw ingredients and ask a chef to cook them with a sauce. It's quite an experience waching four chefs juggling their woks and lots of colourful vegetables! You take your selection of dishes to your table, and the staff colect them when you have finished. The décor is in (9) .... shades of blue and green and easy on the eye, and there is usually some (10) .... oriental music playing in the background. The atmosphere is therefore very relaxing, and people will be able to talk comfortabley with each other.

To sum up, I can thoroughly endorse both restaurants, and I'm sure either would be a huge success with a group of trainees.

Reading and Use of English | Part 8

You are going to read an essay about travel writing. For questions **1–10**, choose from the sections (**A–E**). The sections may be chosen more than once.

Which section mentions

an experience so overwhelming it left people speechless?	1
the compelling nature of youthful impressions?	2
travel writing being a useful tool for a writer to express his ideas with?	3
the way in which human beings attempt to understand the world around them?	4
the writer's attempts to emulate his respected peers?	6
the writer's sense of identification with another's vision?	6
something that is unlikely to be missed if it has never been known?	7
the dual motivation behind a writer's exploration of what he sees?	8
how a gifted travel writer may change the perception of his craft?	9
a contrast between two responses to the world?	10

TRAVEL WRITING

John Brinnin is an American who has been inspired to travel and to write about travel since he was a child. This is an extract from one of his essays.

A Great travel writing is infused with a sense of wonder. A phenomenon that cannot be conclusively defined, it remains best comprehended by its effects. A great narrative of travel is the product of a writer for whom the given subject is but a convenient focus – a chance to draw upon a personal vision that exists before and after any number of its expressions. Unfortunately, a sense of wonder cannot be taught or learnt. It is rather like a musical sense – if not quite a matter of absolute pitch, then a disposition, something in the genes as different from judgment as the incidence of brown eyes or blue. When it's there, its presence is indisputable; when it's absent, it's not likely to be grieved over.

B Some years ago, I spent a few days in Beirut – one of them on an excursion to Baalbek to see the great temple of the sun associated with its ancient name, Heliopolis. The trip was made in a minibus full of strangers with a Lebanese driver. When our visit to the gigantic ruins was over, we squeezed back into our seats in a stunned silence that seemed the only appropriate response to such awesome magnificence. This spell lasted for many miles, broken, finally, by the muffled syllables with which each of us tried to describe the indescribable.

C In order for the sense of wonder to express itself, it must, professionally speaking, call upon the spirit of investigation. Whereas wonder is a receptive state which simply widens or contracts in response to stimuli, the spirit of investigation is active, charged with curiosity, avid to know how and why things come to be, how they work, to what they may be compared, how they fit into any scheme that may render them comprehensible. It is a spirit concerned with something that can be translated, first for love and then for as much cold cash as may be extracted from the editors of glossy journals. Functioning at its best, the spirit of investigation relates the observer to the observed and makes the exotic familiar.

D By description, measurement, and statistics, the spirit of investigation allows the writer's sense of wonder to go to work. The writer is thus able to unite subjective thoughts with objective evidence, to connect the poetry with the prose and so nudge travel writing away from its current status as a consumer report into a literary genre. And since all travel writing is, inescapably, a form of autobiography, I'd like to cite a few instances, a few fortunate moments when, indulging my own sense of wonder and driven by the spirit of investigation, I tried to find a balance that would justify my pretensions to a place somewhere in the vicinity of those writers whose chronicles of travel experience I most admire.

E Of all the images that passed before my eyes in mid-childhood, two affected me like summonses. One was a colored illustration on the cover of a geography book of the young Christopher Columbus, the man who discovered the Americas, gazing westward from a deepwater dock in Genoa. There, I thought, was a boy no older than me who, just like me, had the whole world in his head and still looked forward to another. The second was a painting of what seemed to me a celestial city. Situated at the conjunction of a river and an ocean, it was the scene of dazzling energy as flotillas of ships steamed in and out, railroad trains snaked across lacework bridges, and airplanes soared above steeples and tall smokestacks. I knew at first glance that in New London, Connecticut, I had seen the city of my dreams.

The Temple of the Sun, Baalbek, Lebanon

Listening | Part 3

▶ 14 You will hear an interview in which a writer called Peter Dell is talking about the Brooklyn Bridge in New York. For questions **1–6**, choose the answer (**A, B, C or D**) which fits best according to what you hear.

1 What always happens to Peter each time he arrives at the bridge?

   A He perceives things more clearly.

   B He experiences a sense of loss.

   C He is reassured by something he looks at.

   D He feels a keen sense of danger.

2 What does Peter become aware of as he walks across the bridge?

   A how vulnerable people on it are

   B how symbolic the bridge is

   C how intrusive the traffic is

   D how important the river is now

3 What surprised Peter about the construction of the Brooklyn Bridge?

   A It was once the longest bridge in the world.

   B Workmen died while they were working on it.

   C It was built from an innovative kind of stone.

   D The weight of the bridge was supported by timber.

4 According to Peter, how do most pedestrians today react to the Brooklyn Bridge?

   A They think it compares favourably with the skyscrapers.

   B They believe it is one of the most beautiful locations in New York.

   C They experience the excitement of seeing something unusual.

   D They feel almost as if they are walking on air.

5 What does Peter say about the crimes committed involving the Brooklyn Bridge?

   A Some murders have taken place there.

   B The wires on the bridge were damaged.

   C There has been one minor explosion.

   D Some confidence tricks were successful.

6 According to Peter, what special quality does the bridge have today?

   A It is sheltered from the worst of the winter weather.

   B It is possible to experience brief moments of silence there.

   C It makes you feel as though you are never alone.

   D Its height above the river makes you feel superior.

The living world

Grammar
Countable and uncountable nouns

1 Underline the ten abstract words in this list of uncountable nouns. Then use them to complete sentences 1-10 below.

advice   cereal   charm   education   fruit   glass
information   intelligence   knowledge   luggage
paper   petrol   progress   research   rice   soap
stone   talent   work

1 To my ...knowledge... the documents you require were dispatched well before midday.
2 Rapid .... has been made in recent years in the prevention of malaria.
3 Robert was always able to turn on the .... when a situation became difficult.
4 Joanna was always totally professional when she applied herself to her ....
5 Learning to read at the age of three was an obvious sign of Tom's level of ....
6 My boss always gave very sound .... to younger members of the team.
7 My sister's .... for singing was obvious from an early age.
8 Little .... is available about the ruined castle in the centre of the town.
9 I've always thought that the .... you receive at an early age is the key to success in life.
10 Current .... into arthritis should lead to the development of a new drug.

Verbs followed by prepositions

2a The verbs in the box below are all followed by prepositions. Write them in the correct column.

adapt   apply   base   believe   compliment
concentrate   contribute   decide   depend   donate
engage   focus   impact   insist   participate   react
refer   result   thrive

IN	ON	TO
		adapt

b Choose one of the verbs from the box to go in each sentence and put it into the correct form.

1 She gave an amusing and informative talk without once ...referring... to her notes.
2 My manager .... me on the way I'd handled the situation.
3 The new entry requirements will only be .... to students in certain departments.
4 Some people seem to .... on constant stress whereas for others it causes problems.
5 If you .... in yourself, you'll come across as much more confident.

3 Choose one word to go in each pair of sentences. In one of the sentences the word is countable and in the other it is uncountable so you may need to put it in the correct form to fit the meaning.

difficulty   experience   painting   reason   weight   work

1 a A huge amount of ...work... has gone into this drawing.
  b There are a number of well-known .... of art which the gallery is trying to buy at the moment.
2 a The heat presented Shona with little .... because she'd been brought up in Malaysia.
  b The .... they encountered were so great they abandoned the attempt to cross the channel in canoes.
3 a I was advised to do some training with .... to build up my strength.
  b I was amazed at how much .... I'd put on during the trip.
4 a As soon as I took up .... I got completely absorbed in it and spent all day in my studio.
  b I produced such a large number of .... that I had to give some away.
5 a I enjoyed hearing about Ali's different .... as road manager for a band.
  b I know from .... that there's no point getting angry with Oliver.
6 a I never understood what Steve's .... were for leaving the company.
  b Lara suddenly ran out of the room for no obvious ....

Articles

4 Read this extract from a website and then complete the gaps, using the correct form of the article, *a*, *an*, *the* or ø.

The Global Importance of Coffee

Over **(1)** ...the... last three hundred years coffee has made its way around **(2)** .... world, establishing itself in **(3)** .... economies and lifestyles of **(4)** .... main trading nations. Coffee is now one of **(5)** .... most valuable primary commodities in **(6)** .... world, often second in **(7)** .... value only to **(8)** .... oil as **(9)** .... source of foreign exchange to **(10)** .... developing countries. Millions of people earn their living from **(11)** .... coffee industry.

At times in **(12)** .... history coffee has been hailed as **(13)** .... medicinal cure-all, and at others condemned as **(14)** .... evil brew. In the latter case this was usually for **(15)** .... political or religious reasons, when **(16)** .... coffee houses were at their height of popularity as **(17)** .... meeting places. However, in **(18)** .... last half-century, scientific research has established **(19)** .... facts about coffee, caffeine and our health: in moderation coffee consumption is in no way **(20)** .... health risk; indeed drinking coffee can confer some health benefits.

Vocabulary
Word building

Complete the table below. Write in the missing abstract noun or verb form. Put an asterisk (*) by the words which have the same form in the verb and noun form.

VERB	NOUN	VERB	NOUN
condemn		applaud	applause
consume			defence
create			definition
date*	date		delight
emit			economy
inscribe			experience
presume			function
portray			industry
recover			practice
research			supply
survive			suspect

Writing | Part 2
A proposal

1 Read the proposal on page 61 quickly. What is being suggested, and to whom?

2 Read the proposal again and put one of the linking/referencing words or phrases below in each gap. Use each one only once.

> an additional measure   however   in which
> itself   one final step   such   them
> therefore   these   this   thus   which

3 There are four verbs in the passive form in the proposal. Find them and underline them.

4 Think of a brief heading for each of the four main paragraphs.

Unit 12

Introduction

The purpose of this proposal is to suggest ways (1) ....in which...... cycling provision in the city could be improved. I will suggest a range of measures to achieve this.

A ....

There is already a series of cycle tracks leading from the 'park and ride' car parks around the city. (2) .... has encouraged local people to see their bicycles as a valid means of transport, (3) .... has in turn brought enormous benefits in terms of the environment. There remain, (4) ...., a number of further improvements to be made by the council.

B ....

The first of (5) .... is a major reorganisation of the traffic flow. Our city is historic, with narrow streets; it is dangerous to maintain two-way traffic on (6) .... roads and adding a cycle lane simply compounds the problem. I (7) .... suggest that a one-way system is introduced at the earliest possible opportunity.

C ....

(8) .... that would bring rapid results is if businesses provided secure bicycle storage on their premises and also showers on site and even loans to buy bicycles. That would mean employees would have an incentive to cycle to work.

D ....

(9) .... would be to offer bicycles for daily hire in the historic city centre (10) ...., at a rate that would be appealing to tourists, and also to offer (11) .... as an option at the park and ride car parks, (12) .... taking pressure off the bus system too.

Conclusion

I believe that if all the suggested measures were implemented, cycling in the city would soon become the transport of choice for most people.

Reading and Use of English | Part 4

For questions **1–6**, complete the second sentence so that it has a similar meaning to the first sentence, using the word given. Here is an example (**0**).

Example:

0 I do not intend to stay in my present job very much longer.
POSSIBILITY
There is ....no possibility of me staying............ in my present job very much longer.

1 We should leave about six, otherwise we might not get there in time for dinner.
SET
If .... by six, we might not get there in time for dinner.

2 Kim and Sara agreed that the lecture was the best one they had ever attended.
BETTER
Kim and Sara agreed that they had .... lecture.

3 I discovered that the man I sat next to at the planning meeting was a member of the council.
TURNED
The man I sat next to at the planning meeting .... a member of the council.

4 There is no point in tidying the room before we've finished decorating.
SENSE
It makes .... the room before we've finished decorating.

5 Tony rarely says much when our group is discussing things.
PARTICIPATES
Tony hardly .... our group discussions.

6 The bus driver admitted causing the accident at the crossroads.
BLAME
The bus driver .... the accident at the crossroads.

Reading and Use of English | Part 1

For questions **1–8**, read the text below and decide which answer (**A, B, C** or **D**) best fits each gap. There is an example at the beginning (**0**).

Example:

0   A originate   B belong   C date   D exist

The Beauty of the Beasts

The earliest known drawings, which survive in caves in Western Europe, (0) .... back about 30,000 years. The fact that some people (1) .... considerable distances along underground passages in (2) .... darkness to create them is evidence that producing such pictures was an (3) .... of great importance to these artists.

But what was their purpose? Perhaps drawing was an essential part of the ceremonials enacted to bring success in hunting. Perhaps the paintings were intended not to (4) .... the death of the creatures portrayed but, (5) ...., to ensure their fertility, and thus a good supply of meat. The only certainty is that these drawings are assured, accurate and breathtakingly beautiful.

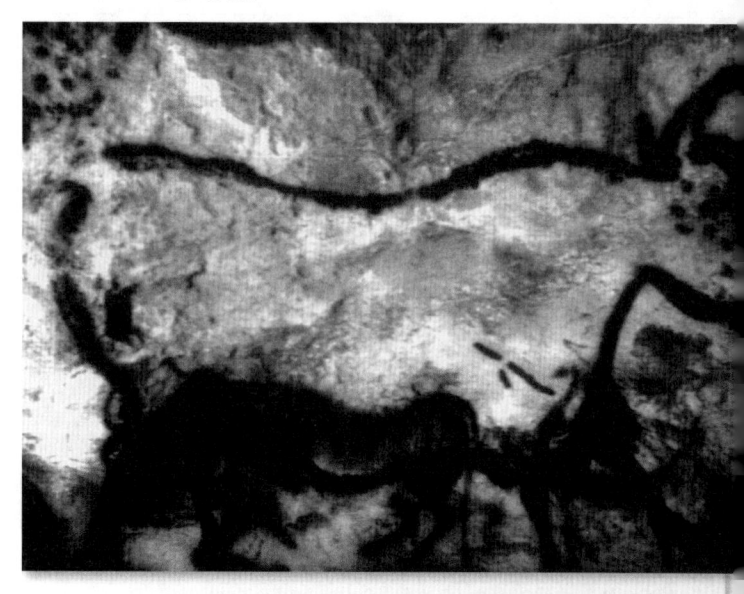

This practice of painting (6) .... of animals on walls continued throughout our history. Five thousand years ago, when people in Egypt built the world's first cities, they too inscribed animals on their walls. There is, however, no (7) .... about the function of these: the Egyptians (8) .... animals as gods.

1	A approached	B crawled	C dragged	D proceeded
2	A whole	B entire	C full	D complete
3	A act	B impact	C operation	D effect
4	A take over	B bring about	C put forward	D make out
5	A in contrast	B on the contrary	C not at all	D on the other hand
6	A aspects	B appearances	C reflections	D images
7	A suspicion	B reason	C mistrust	D doubt
8	A celebrated	B praised	C worshipped	D adored

Listening | Part 1

▶ 15 You will hear three different extracts. For questions **1–6**, choose the answer (**A**, **B** or **C**) which fits best according to what you hear. There are two questions for each extract.

Extract One

You hear part of a radio discussion about Monarch butterflies.

1 According to the man, in what way do Monarch butterflies differ from other butterflies?
   A They fly very long distances.
   B They spend the winter in a warm climate.
   C They survive best at high altitude.

2 What does the man find surprising about Monarch butterflies?
   A They can only migrate once.
   B They migrate in large groups.
   C They migrate to a precise location.

Extract Two

You hear two friends talking about the final of a cookery competition they saw on television.

3 They agree that the winning contestant
   A performed well at a crucial moment.
   B fully deserved to win the contest.
   C used an intriguing range of ingredients.

4 The woman thinks that yesterday's cookery programme could be improved by
   A adding a new person to the judges' panel.
   B varying the format of the presentation.
   C specifying what style of cooking contestants must do.

Extract Three

You hear two friends discussing a trip to a game park in South Africa.

5 Before the woman went to South Africa, the man had told her that
   A the sheer size of the animals would be impressive.
   B the game park would be the highlight of the trip.
   C the sunsets were spectacular in this kind of landscape.

6 The woman thought the elephant approached their jeep because
   A it wanted to warn them off.
   B it was searching for food.
   C it was simply curious.

13 Health and lifestyle

Grammar
The language of comparison

1 Look at the photographs and then write sentences comparing them, using the comparison words in brackets.

1 (less) The people rafting are having a less relaxing time.
2 (much) ....
3 (not so) ....
4 (fewer) ....
5 (a great deal) ....
6 (by far) ....

2 ▶16 Read what a student said about the photographs and then complete the gaps, using the conjunctions and adverbs in the box below. You will need to use some of them more than once. Then listen and check your answers.

> although   but   despite   even if   however   ~~whereas~~

The people in the top picture look as though they're having to work really hard. That's probably because white-water rafting tends to be a very serious hobby (1) ....whereas.... rowing can be enjoyed by anyone. Some people won't agree with that, (2) .... , because they'll say you can be very serious about rowing too. I just mean that anyone can go rowing on a lake (3) .... they haven't made any preparations, (4) .... it's more important to plan properly if you go rafting. The weather can change suddenly in the mountains and it doesn't look very good in this picture. They seem to have decided to go rafting (5) .... the bad weather (6) .... maybe it wasn't like that when they started. These people must have planned their trip properly as they seem to have the right equipment with them. (7) .... rafting can be quite dangerous, some people have been known to attempt it without the right equipment. I've only ever been rafting once – we didn't have all the right things and I got really scared. After that, I decided rafting wasn't for me. I wouldn't go again (8) .... you paid me!

64

Vocabulary
Word building

1 Read this short article about allergies and then put the words in brackets into the correct form.

Allergies: their causes and treatment

The number of people in Britain receiving a new
(1) ....diagnosis.... (*diagnose*) of allergies such as asthma, eczema and hay fever is increasing by five per cent every year.

There is some **(2)** .... (*evident*) to show that Britain's **(3)** .... (*obsess*) with rules and regulations to ensure cleanliness in the home, supermarket and workplace is reflected in the number of allergy **(4)** .... (*suffer*). One theory is that we have far less **(5)** .... (*expose*) to dirt and germs during childhood than we used to have, so our bodies do not have the opportunity to develop a **(6)** .... (*resist*) to allergens. While we may look down on the totally **(7)** .... (*hygiene*) approach to food and general living which people had in the past, there are some lessons we could learn today by maybe being a bit less **(8)** .... (*caution*).

Nobody would dispute the importance of **(9)** .... (*clinic*) advances. These include vaccinations given routinely to children, which have given several generations **(10)** .... (*free*) from anxiety about catching some life-threatening diseases. However, despite the obvious benefits of protecting against some diseases, vaccinations for less serious diseases can be **(11)** .... (*controversy*). Discussion continues over whether they actually **(12)** .... (*weak*) our immune systems and are being given **(13)** .... (*necessary*) for diseases which are not dangerous. In the meantime, a whole industry has developed around preventative medicines which are very **(14)** .... (*effect*) in treating allergies.

Adjectives followed by prepositions

2 Write the correct preposition in each sentence.

1 I'm not familiar ....with........ Sydney so I can't recommend the best places to go.
2 I'm always extremely generous .... my brother.
3 I'm not very tolerant .... people who talk loudly on their mobiles in the train.
4 Sarah isn't capable .... cooking a meal for everybody without help.
5 My parents are hopeless .... art but my sister and I are both artists now.
6 Simon has lived in Finland and is very knowledgeable .... the country's history.
7 Paul is very efficient .... making travel arrangements.
8 I suddenly became aware .... someone standing next to me.

Expressions with parts of the body

3a Choose a part of the body to complete these idiomatic expressions. Use some of the words more than once.

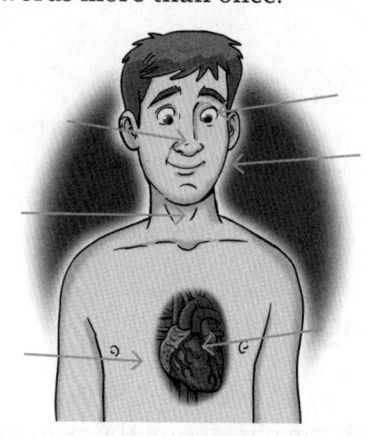

1 I knew the children shouldn't play in the trees but they were having such a good time I turned a blind ....eye........ .
2 Every time I read that poem it brings a lump to my ....
3 She leaves the country and breaks his .... at the end of the film.
4 By doing two jobs I manage to keep my .... above water.
5 I had to get it off my .... and tell my friend what was annoying me.
6 He's in the public .... so has to be careful what he says and to whom.
7 She turned her .... up at the restaurant I had chosen as it wasn't in a smart part of town.
8 After not getting anywhere with her applications to drama school she lost .... and decided to be a lawyer.

b Now match each idiomatic expression above to its meaning.

A to stop believing you can succeed ....8....
B to have just enough money to live on ....
C to tell someone something that's concerned you for some time ....
D to not accept something which you think is not good enough ....
E to make someone else feel very sad ....
F to be famous and often featured in the media ....
G to choose to ignore something ....
H to make you feel a strong emotion ....

Health and lifestyle

Illness and health

4 Choose a verb from the box to complete each phrase.

> blow catch clear develop feel fracture hold
> lose pull ~~suffer~~

1 to ..suffer.. from asthma
2 to .... your nose when you have a cold
3 to .... your voice when you have a sore throat
4 to .... your breath underwater
5 to .... an allergy suddenly
6 to .... a bone in your wrist
7 to .... a cold from someone
8 to .... your throat before you speak
9 to .... a muscle while running
10 to .... a sharp pain in your knee

Writing | Part 2
A letter

1a Match the phrases on the right to a function on the left. Some functions have more than one phrase.

giving an opinion	A to summarise
persuading	B some people argue that … but others
summing up	C in my point of view
comparing and contrasting	D I would be grateful if you could let me know
recommending and advising	E the benefits of doing this are
asking for advice or help	F I would be more than happy to
making an offer	G the main advantage for you is
describing	H in conclusion,
	I on the one hand … (on the other hand)
	J it would be a good idea to
	K I would like to know what
	L I think it would definitely
	M is an essential feature of

b Read the letter.
Who is Tina Brown?
Why is she writing this letter?
What does she hope to achieve?

c Use some of the phrases above to complete the gaps.

Dear Sir/Madam,

I am writing on behalf of all members about the extremely poor state of the showers and changing rooms at the tennis club. **(1)** ......K...... you intend to do about them.

At present everything is in a very dilapidated condition, and the supply of hot water is constantly running out. In our opinion, **(2)** .... completely refurbish the showers. **(3)** .... that current members will be much more content with the facilities, while in addition, having state-of-the-art showers and a pleasant décor **(4)** .... any club hoping to attract new members in competitive times.

I appreciate that **(5)** .... the refurbishment will require major investment, but on the other there are long-term benefits, both financial and practical. I would have to say, however, that **(6)** .... putting an end to the constant flow of complaints you receive from us all.

(7) .... when the management committee will be able to discuss these matters. Please note that **(8)** .... come and discuss them with you if it would be helpful. Most of the players at the club live locally, and wish to continue their membership.

Yours

Tina Brown

Reading and Use of English | Part 6

You are going to read the views of four scientists on the effects of sport participation on young athletes. For questions 1–4, choose from texts **A–D**. They may be chosen more than once.

Sport: A Positive Influence

Four scientists report on the findings of their investigations into the well-being of young athletes

A

The young athletes interviewed seemed emotionally resilient and able to cope with the pressures of the training and performance environments. In this they appeared helped by their family environment and parental interest, with very few of them experiencing persistent tension or anxiety about the prospect of training or competing. Furthermore, the rate of self-reported psychological illness was lower amongst these athletes than in the general population, which must relate to the cohesion which is an obvious characteristic of athletic families. It is not possible to say whether young athletes enter and persist in sport because of their positive family and psychological characteristics, or whether the reverse is the case, with involvement in sport having a positive effect on mood and family function. Nonetheless, as all athletes know, close attention to diet and nutrition is a prerequisite and makes an obvious contribution to well-being.

B

My findings suggest that intensive training had a significant effect on the young athlete and his or her family where leisure time and friendships were concerned. These youngsters devoted a considerable amount of free time to training, but not to the extent that it affected their ability to make and retain key relationships. Training was seen as a positive aspect of their lives rather than increasing their stress levels. In addition, the advantages of intensive training to physical health appeared major, with young athletes rarely experimenting with smoking and eating sensibly being the norm. Unfortunately, because of the cost of accessing sports programmes, it appeared that the positive gains were not equally open to all classes and family types. However, young athletes perceived their families to be more supportive and more willing to embrace change than youngsters who were not participating in sport.

C

Rates of emotional and behavioural problems within a population of young athletes and a group of control youngsters were compared in our survey. Over two-thirds described their daily health as above average, with few actually experiencing poor health. Tension levels, however, were higher among young athletes who feel the pressure on them but they are well trained to handle this. The pattern of medication use and symptom reporting does suggest some degree of physical illness, but certainly not to the extent that it significantly affected general health status. One could conceivably go as far as to speculate that young athletes have more resilience to illness and infection than those who are non-participants; it is however, not known whether this is because of the social incentives and reinforcement practices of the coach or parent involved, or because intense sporting activity in fact affords a measure of protection from illness.

D

As we sampled our sports group, we found that two-thirds of them described their health as significantly above average. Very few appeared to experience poor health during the study. Most interestingly, many young athletes reported a minimal amount of nerves or anxiety during training. Those who had this reaction experienced only the mildest of symptoms, usually characterised by feelings of restlessness. Additionally, the close family environment played a pivotal role in protection against psychological illness. Interestingly, the athletes perceived their families to be closer, more nurturing and more adaptable in their approach than did a comparable group of youngsters. However, some concern was felt about athletes' siblings, who occasionally struggle to accept the success of an elite athlete within the family and may even on occasion feel neglected by parents.

1 Which writer expresses a different view from the others about the psychological effects of participating in a sport?

2 Which two writers express uncertainty about the relationship between two factors?

3 Which writer shares writer A's view that participating in sport encourages the adoption of a healthy lifestyle?

4 Which two writers express a similar view on the flexible attitudes found in athletes' families?

Health and lifestyle

Listening | Part 2

▶17 You will hear a sports trainer called Bradley Robbins talking to a group of sports science students about his job with a professional basketball team. For questions **1-8**, complete the sentences with a word or short phrase.

TRAINING A BASKETBALL TEAM

Bradley says that lack of [1] _____ causes most problems in a team.

From his studies, Bradley finds what he learnt about the [2] _____ particularly useful.

Bradley finds injuries to players' [3] _____ are the most common.

Bradley dismisses most of the new ideas about ways of increasing [4] _____ as unhelpful.

Bradley says exercises focusing on improving [5] _____ are the most effective.

Bradley advises players about [6] _____ to help them recover after a match.

Bradley tries to match his approach to the particular [7] _____ in the team.

According to Bradley, it is absolutely essential to have a [8] _____ if you want to succeed as a trainer.

14 Moving abroad

Grammar
Emphasis: cleft sentences

1 Read each pair of sentences and then complete the gap in the second sentence.

1 George didn't have anywhere to live over the summer so he rented a caravan by the beach.

   George didn't have anywhere to live over the summer so what **he did was rent** .... a caravan by the beach.

2 The local football team need a good manager to help them achieve their potential.

   All .... to help them achieve their potential.

3 I decided to apply to this college because of the excellent sports facilities.

   It was because of .... this college.

4 I want to save enough money to take flying lessons.

   What .... flying lessons.

5 Every morning he checks his emails before he does anything else.

   The first thing .... his emails.

6 If your credit card is stolen, you should ring the emergency number immediately.

   What .... the emergency number immediately.

7 Sue gave up her acting career because she needed a steady income.

   The reason .... she needed a steady income.

8 We must avoid upsetting her at the moment.

   The worst thing to .... to upset her.

Intensifying adverbs

2 Complete these sentences by choosing the adverb in *italics* which forms a collocation with the adjective which follows.

1 I'm (*absolutely*) / *extremely* certain that I didn't leave my key in the lock.
2 Peter was *totally* / *dreadfully* disappointed when he didn't get offered a place on the expedition.
3 We were each served a fish to eat which was *simply* / *very* enormous.
4 When you see his car, you'll agree with me that our neighbour must be *really* / *utterly* rich.
5 The film was *entirely* / *hugely* entertaining.
6 The view from our balcony is *very* / *absolutely* wonderful.
7 It's *incredibly* / *perfectly* normal to feel anxious before performing in a concert.
8 Waiting for a bus in the rain is *utterly* / *entirely* depressing.

Comment adverbials

3 Add an adverb from the box below to each sentence. Do not change the form of any of the words.

admittedly   coincidentally   typically   up to a point
wisely   ~~wrongly~~

1 The chauffeur was *wrongly* accused of giving the newspapers the story when in fact he knew nothing about it.

2 The organisers of the marathon changed the start of the race from 11 am to 7 am because of the heat.

3 Ruth named her baby Amber and her cousin in Australia chose the same name for her baby.

4 I agree with you that technology makes our lives easier but it also means we can never properly relax.

5 I got the job because my father is managing director.

6 We were taken to eat in a village restaurant where the food they served was Portuguese rather than an international mix.

Moving abroad

4a Underline the comment adverbials in these sentences.

1. Personally, I see no reason why Kamila shouldn't get a place to study medicine next year.
   ....

2. We were obviously thrilled to hear we'd got lottery funding to build a new community centre.
   ....

3. Generally speaking, new children settle very quickly into the school.
   ....

4. Apparently, Nadia's cousin has decided to give up her job and go home.
   ....

b For each of the sentences above, choose the group of three comment adverbials from the box below which have a similar meaning to the one in the sentence. Write them under the sentence.

> as a rule   as far as I'm concerned   as I see it
> clearly   for the most part   from what I've heard
> it goes without saying   It seems that   needless to say
> on the whole   or so I'm told   to my mind

c Use one of the phrases in the box to help you rewrite the sentences below.

1. Alex was clearly delighted to be given the chance to work in San Francisco.

   It goes .... delighted to be given the chance to work in San Francisco.

2. Apparently, they've changed the rules about who needs a visa.

   It .... changed about who needs a visa.

3. Generally speaking, nearly all of the fruit eaten today in Britain has travelled long distances.

   For .... fruit eaten today in Britain has travelled long distances.

4. To my mind, buying cheap clothes is a waste of time as they don't last.

   As .... is a waste of time buying cheap clothes as they don't last.

Vocabulary

Living in another country

Complete the crossword on page 71 by using these clues.

Across

2. In periods of unemployment there is fierce .... for jobs and recent immigrants may lose out.
3. Countries with a booming .... tend to attract immigrants.
6. There is a desperate .... for a new school due to the arrival of new immigrants in the area.
9. Britain is increasingly a .... society with people from a wide range of backgrounds.
11. The .... of immigrants into the local community is crucial.
12. Cultural .... brings a variety of new ideas to a community in terms of customs and outlook.
13. I missed my family and felt .... for the first few weeks.
14. .... in the language helps immigrants find work and settle.

Down

1. I'm a .... to this town and I haven't got used to finding my way around yet.
3. There are people from more than 30 .... groups living in this neighbourhood.
4. The .... country for the next World Cup will be chosen next week.
5. My parents emigrated when they were children with their aunts, grandparents, cousins – in fact, their whole .... family.
7. Most countries have strict limits on .... levels.
8. Making the .... into a new society can be difficult.
10. It is important to respect other cultures and show .... towards different customs.

Writing | Part 1
An essay

1 Read the essay below about the benefits of living in a multicultural city.

  a Choose the correct word to complete the phrase or sentence.
  b Ten words in the essay are spelled wrongly. Find them and correct them.

It is living in a (1) *truly* / *widely* cosmopolitane city that has made me realise just how important culturall diversity is. What (2) *enhances* / *enriches* a society is the huge energie and enthusiasm that newcomers to the country bring. It is (3) *since* / *because* they are starting afresh, looking at everything for the first time, that you question your own values and aproach to life, particularly in the workplace. And to be (4) *honest* / *open*, the new workers who arrive are, as a (5) *rule* / *whole*, often prepared to do (6) *absolutely* / *totally* mundane jobs until they become better etablished, and can set their sights (7) *utterly* / *really* high.

On a (8) *realistic* / *positive* note, having different ethnicities within a city means benefitting from an (9) *absolutely* / *extremely* vibrante cultural life as well; different groups will bring in new music, theatre and of course cuisine. As I (10) *call* / *see* it, whole neighbourhoods spring up around this culture, making each part of the city a different expirience. It makes for an (11) *incredibly* / *absolutely* exciting and diverse background, and a (12) *very* / *simply* enjoyable existance.

Consequently, all I want is to see these diverse ethnic groups (13) *thrive* / *advance* within our city, creating a new generation with (14) *completely* / *utterly* tolerant views of each other, and common ties to our country and its future. As far as I am (15) *involved* / *concerned*, this is quite simpley the only way forward in the next century. It is living and working together that (16) *develops* / *progresses* true harmony and integration.

Reading and Use of English | Part 2

For questions **1–8**, read the text below and think of the word which best fits each gap. Use only **one** word in each gap. There is an example at the beginning (**0**).

Ellis Island

Over twelve million immigrants entered the United States (**0**) ...*between*... 1892 and 1954 through Ellis Island, the first Federal Immigration Station. Annie Moore, a 15 year-old Irish girl, entered history and a new country as (**1**) .... very first immigrant to be processed there in 1892. Over the next 62 years, many more immigrants (**2**) .... to follow through this port of entry and go (**3**) .... to make new lives in their adopted country. (**4**) .... most of them then spread across the country, it is estimated that (**5**) .... to fifty per cent of all Americans can trace at least one family member who passed through Ellis Island on arrival.

Following a major restoration project, the main building on the island was reopened to the public in 1990 as the Ellis Island Immigration Museum. Nearly a century (**6**) .... the peak years of immigration, it is (**7**) .... of the most popular tourist destinations and receives almost two million visitors annually, many of (**8**) .... take the opportunity to find out about their ancestors.

Reading and Use of English | Part 3

For questions **1–8**, read the text below. Use the word given in capitals at the end of some of the lines to form a word that fits in the gap in the same line. There is an example at the beginning (**0**).

Advice to families moving abroad

When a family moves to a new country they need to think about how to maintain their own language and (**0**) ...*encourage*... their children to learn a new one. Not (**1**) .... the experience of being dropped into a group of people who do not speak their language can be (**2**) .... for children. There will be moments when the children need (**3**) .... from their parents and it may be more crucial than ever to maintain routines which are (**4**) .... important such as story-telling in the home language. These routines emphasise the permanence of the (**5**) .... between parent and child.
It is (**6**) .... not to start speaking the new language to the child at home. The importance to the child of associating parental relations with one particular language should not be (**7**) .... and one can easily imagine how stress at school coupled with a sudden switch of language at home may be interpreted by the child as a kind of (**8**) ...., particularly at a moment of general upheaval for the whole family.

COURAGE
SURPRISE
PUZZLE
REASSURE

EMOTION
RELATION

PREFER

ESTIMATE

DENY

Listening | Part 2

17 You will hear a man called Adam Campbell talking to a group of young business people about his experience of going to live and work in Romania. For questions **1–8**, complete the sentences with a word or short phrase.

LIVING AND WORKING IN ROMANIA

Adam's wife is Romanian and he was recently offered a job as [1] _____ in Romania.

His wife found a flat but then they had to buy [2] _____ in a hurry.

Where climate is concerned, he finds the [3] _____ more difficult to deal with than he expected.

Adam and his wife spend leisure time in the mountains where he enjoys [4] _____ .

Adam says [5] _____ is not very good in the part of the city where he lives.

Adam disagrees with people who say that [6] _____ is the best local food.

Because of his poor knowledge of the language, Adam doesn't often go to the [7] _____ .

Adam thinks Romanian people have more [8] _____ for social events than people in Scotland.

Acknowledgements

Development of this publication has made use of the Cambridge English Corpus (CEC). The CEC is a computerised database of contemporary spoken and written English, which currently stands at over one billion words. It includes British English, American English and other varieties of English. It also includes the Cambridge Learner Corpus, developed in collaboration with Cambridge English Language Assessment. Cambridge University Press has built up the CEC to provide evidence about language use that helps to produce better language learning materials.

The authors and publishers acknowledge the following sources of copyright material and are grateful for the permissions granted. While every effort has been made, it has not always been possible to identify the sources of all the material used, or to trace all copyright holders. If any omissions are brought to our notice, we will be happy to include the appropriate acknowledgements on reprinting.

The publisher has used its best endeavours to ensure that the URLs for external websites referred to in this book are correct and active at the time of going to press. However, the publisher has no responsibility for the websites and can make no guarantee that a site will remain live or that the content is or will remain appropriate.

Text
Penguin Books Limited and David Godwin Associates for the text on p. 6 adapted from *The Farm* by Richard Benson, published by Hamish Hamilton, 2005. Copyright © Richard Benson 2005. Reproduced by permission of Penguin Books Limited and David Godwin Associates;

Psych Central for text B on p. 17 adapted from 'Book Review: Smart Thinking by Art Markman' by Dave Schultz, *Psych Central*, http://psychcentral.com/lib/book-review-smart-thinking/00015721. Reproduced with permission;

Max Read for text C on p. 17 adapted from 'Smart Thinking: Three Essential Keys to Solve Problems, Innovate, and Get Things Done by Art Markman' by Max Read, *Goodreads*. Reproduced with permission;

Lisa Belkin for the text on p. 21 adapted from 'Life's Work: Putting Some Fun Back Into 9 to 5' by Lisa Belkin, *The New York Times*, 6 March 2008. Reproduced by permission of Lisa Belkin;

The Daily Telegraph for the text on pp. 26–27 adapted from 'Bob Skeleton: the scariest ride on the planet' by Charles Starmer-Smith, *The Telegraph*, 9 February 2008. Copyright © Telegraph Media Group Limited 2008;

University of Michigan School of Education for the text on p. 41 adapted from 'The Role of Television Viewing in the Development of Reading Comprehension' by Paul van den Broek, 19 June 2001, www.ciera.org/library/archive/2001-02/200102pv.pdf. Reproduced with permission;

Nick T Spark for the text on pp. 46–47 adapted from '46.2 Gs!!! The Story of John Paul Stapp "The Fastest Man on Earth"' by Nick T Spark, http://www.ejectionsite.com/stapp.htm. Reproduced with permission from Nick T Spark;

Text on p. 57 adapted from 'Travel and the Sense of Wonder' by John Brinnin, *Vagablogging*, 1991;

British Coffee Association for the text on p. 60 adapted from 'The History of Coffee', *British Coffee Association*, 13 May 2008. Information Courtesy of the British Coffee Association;

The Daily Telegraph for the text on pp. 62 adapted from 'Beauty of the beasts' by David Attenborough, *The Daily Telegraph*, 24 February 2007. Copyright © Telegraph Media Group Limited 2007;

Text on p. 67 adapted from 'Ruff Guide to the Training of Young Athletes (TOYA)' by T D Sasha, *Sports Development*, 1 January 2013;

Cambridge University Press for the text on p. 72 adapted from *The Bilingual Family 1st edition* by Edith Harding and Philip Riley, published by Cambridge University Press, 1986. Copyright © Cambridge University Press 1986. Reproduced with permission;

Guardian News and Media Ltd for the recording on p. 82, Extract Two adapted from 'It's about what we've created together' by Joanna Moorhead, *The Guardian*, 9 February 2008. Copyright © Guardian News & Media Ltd 2008.

Photos
p. 4: Visions of America, LLC / Alamy; p. 6 (L): Adrian Sherratt/Alamy; p. 6 (R): THE FARM: THE STORY OF ONE FAMILY AND THE ENGLISH COUNTRYSIDE by Richard Benson (Hamish Hamilton 2005, 2006). Cover reproduced with permission from Penguin Ltd. p. 8: Cultura/Rex Features; p. 9 (T): Artmin/Shutterstock; p. 9 (B): SnowWhiteimages/Shutterstock; p. 14: Flaming June, c.1895 (oil on canvas) by Leighton, Frederic (1830-96) Museo de Arte, Ponce, Puerto Rico, West Indies/ © The Maas Gallery, London, UK/ The Bridgeman Art Library; p. 18: kjorgen/iStock/Thinkstock; p. 19 (L): Wavebreakmedia Ltd/Thinkstock; p. 19 (R): Werner Dietrich/Alamy; p. 21: Blend Images/Alamy; p. 23 (L): Cultura/Rex Features; p. 23 (R): Patti McConville/Getty Images; p. 24: Royal Geographical Society/Alamy; p. 27: Jeff Gilbert/Rex Features; p. 28: Jelle-vd-Wolf/Shutterstock; p. 29: The Thirteenth Tale by Diane Setterfield, The Orion Publishing Group Ltd. p. 31: Tim Sloan/AFP/Getty Images; p. 32: maurice joseph/Alamy; p. 33: sturti/Getty Images; p. 34: Michael Kemp/Alamy; p. 35: Ragnarock/Shutterstock; p. 36: Lorenzo Fanchi/Alamy; p. 38: Bettina Strenske/Alamy; p. 39: www.railimages.co.uk; p. 41: Niamh Baldock/Alamy; p. 43: marc macdonald/Alamy; p. 44: RA/Lebrecht Music & Arts Library; p. 46: Courtesy of the Air Force Flight Test Center History Office p. 48: Suzi Eszterhas/Minden Pictures/FLPA; p. 50: H. Mark Weidman Photography/Alamy; p. 51: Courtesy of Boston College, MA, USA p. 52: Andreas Rodriguez/Thinkstock; p. 53: UPPA/Photoshot; p. 54: turtix/iStock/Thinkstock; p. 57: Mahler Attar/Sygma/Corbis p. 58: Bettmann/Corbis; p. 60: dirkr/Getty Images; p. 62: Ray Roberts/Alamy; p. 63: Purestock/Punchstock/Getty Images; p. 64 (BL): Alex Segre/Alamy; p. 64 (TR): VCL/Tim Barnett/Getty Images; p. 64 (BR): Digital Vision/Punchstock/Getty Images; p. 68: Jupiterimages/Thinkstock; p. 70: Janine Wiedel/Rex Features; p. 72 (T): Roger-Viollet/Rex Features; p. 72 (B): Robert Harding Picture Library/Superstock; p. 73: iStockphoto.com/Remus Eserblom.

Cover image: Aleksandr Markin/Shutterstock (front, back).

Illustration acknowledgements
Dusan Paulic (Beehive Illustration) p. 5, 65

The publishers are grateful to the following contributors:
Brigit Viney: project management
Sarah Curtis: editorial work
Ainara Solara: proofreader
Kevin Brown: picture research
Leon Chambers: audio producer

Designed and typeset by Wild Apple Design Ltd
Audio recorded at Soundhouse studios, London